KS English

WRITING
FICTION & NON-FICTION

Test Revision Guide

Teacher Book
with Copymasters

Pie Corbett & Ann Webley

Contents

Badger Publishing

Introduction

KEY STAGE 1 WRITING TESTS

What is this book for?

The book provides a bank of materials that would be useful for any year 2 teacher wishing to teach fiction, non-fiction or poetry.

The book contains:

- Models for children to read and discuss with their teacher.
- Samples for the teacher to use when demonstrating.
- Writing toolkits which summarise the structure and language features needed for different kinds of writing.
- Help with planning writing.
- Suggestions for oral activities and paired or group activities to support each unit.
- Assessment suggestions in line with key stage 1 SATs tests.

Young writers flourish in an atmosphere that excites their imagination. Therefore, it is especially important to use a variety of stimuli, alongside the texts, to help develop their ideas for writing and their use of language. Some useful suggestions:

- Snatches of music to help create atmosphere or mood.
- Objects to trigger a story – an old box, a rusty key, a shiny pebble – the list is endless.
- A tape of sound effects – footsteps, a creaking door, etc.

Play word association games in quick five minute bursts to help develop vocabulary. This works for the same reason as frequent and intensive phonics activities.

How to use this book

There is a suggested pattern to using the units within this book, though, of course, teachers will adapt different units to suits the needs of their pupils. Our suggested approach for each teaching unit is as follows.

A. Reading as a writer

1. Read and discuss the model text. Ask the children to discuss what type of writing this is, thinking about the purpose and audience.

2. Get the children to work out how the text is structured. Use questioning techniques that allow the children to solve problems that you set. If they are able to see the structure for themselves, they will be in a better position to copy it in their own writing. The texts are all complete to help this process. Begin to build up a "Writer's Toolkit" with rules about the structure. These will be in a very simple form and will be developed and added to as children read more complex examples of stories and non-fiction text types in Key Stage 2.

3. Now use questioning to draw out the language features of the text. Add these to the class "Writer's toolkit". Wherever possible, let the children tell you what they notice – avoid the temptation to tell them. There is a 'Writer's Toolkit' included with each unit.

4. Once the children have understood the structure and the features, a list should be on display in the classroom and constantly referred to.

5. It is also a good idea to create on-going toolkits for writing sentences. These would relate to any unit being studied and might include reminders about capital letters, punctuation marks and the words making sense on their own.

6. You may like to give children a small photocopied section from a text to see if they can find a certain feature. Children like underlining or circling in colour and the exercise helps them to internalise what they are learning.

B. Teaching writing

1. The units contain oral activities which can be slotted in at any point during the block of work. It is essential to give children a lot of opportunities to talk through ideas, to role play, to gossip as characters, to give each other clear oral instructions. It is part of the process which creates a good writer.

2. There are also practice activities – often in the form of games - which focus on the kind of sentence level objectives which children need to get to grips with for success. Once again, these should be slotted in at appropriate points of the unit and can be repeated and amended as required.

3. The teacher should now use the 'Writer's Toolkit' and "model" writing, using the structure and features in the 'Writer's Toolkit'. Explain the thinking behind the writing like a running commentary as you write. Each unit provides at least one text for demonstration purposes. Annotated versions of these texts are also provided to indicate the features you may wish to draw to the children's attention. Provide lots of opportunities for the children to join in by talking to response partners or writing an idea for a word on their whiteboard. After the demonstration, the children could write something similar, either in sections as you write or as a piece of extended writing.

The SATs Tests

In May 2003, changes were made to the way English is assessed at Key Stage 1. Although it seems that a greater emphasis will soon be placed upon a teacher's judgement about the ability of children, the written tests are set to continue.

Children will complete two set writing tasks, one longer and one shorter. They can only be taken once. The tests are not strictly timed as at Key Stage 2, but after the introduction and time allowed for planning, the longer task is likely to take about 45 minutes and the shorter task about 30 minutes. Teachers will continue to have scope to decide the exact content of the task within a set parameter.

Writing assessment focuses

QCA state that the two writing prompts will target different purposes and forms of writing to give a range of evidence for the writing level. Examples of planning formats will be provided for the longer task, but it is not a requirement to use them.

The aspects of writing to be assessed are children's ability to:

- write imaginative, interesting and thoughtful texts;
- produce texts which are appropriate to task, reader and purpose;

- organise and present whole texts effectively, sequencing and structuring information, ideas and events;
- construct paragraphs and use cohesion within and between paragraphs;
- vary sentences for clarity, purpose and effect;
- write with technical accuracy of syntax and punctuation in phrases, clauses and sentences;
- select appropriate and effective vocabulary;
- use correct spelling.

Marking at key stage 1

Marking now involves making explicit judgements about different aspects of children's writing, rather than a single overall judgement. Marks will first be awarded for sentence level features and will then build up to whole text features in composition and effect.

The longer task will be marked for:

Sentence structure   (*maximum 4 marks*)
- vary sentences for clarity, purpose and effect.

Punctuation   (*maximum 4 marks*)
- write with technical accuracy of syntax and punctuation in phrases, clauses and sentences.

Composition and effect   (*maximum 10 marks*)
- write with imaginative, interesting and thoughtful texts;
- produce texts which are appropriate to task, reader and purpose;
- organise and present whole texts effectively.

For the longer task, composition and effect will include elements of text structure and organisation in the upper bands of the mark scheme, to provide continuity with the fuller evidence obtained from key stage 2. Also for this task, children's ability to construct grammatically accurate sentences will be assessed separately from their control of correct punctuation so that progress in these areas can be monitored precisely.

The shorter task will be marked for:

Sentence structure and punctuation   (*maximum 5 marks*)
- vary sentences for clarity, purpose and effect;
- write with technical accuracy of syntax and punctuation in phrases, clauses and sentences.

Composition and effect   (*maximum 7 marks*)
- write with imaginative, interesting and thoughtful texts;
- produce texts which are appropriate to task, reader and purpose;
- organise and present whole texts effectively.

 **Poetry**

TEACHER'S NOTES

The focus of this section is to develop the children's ability to write poetically. It is important to make sure that there are plenty of poetry books available and children browse and read these. A whole class performance for assembly would be ideal and children should also perform in groups, pairs or solo. This will help them internalise the patterns of poetic language.

Reading as a writer

1. Read and discuss the various models. Try reading them with one half of the class reading aloud while the others listen and then swap roles. Are there favourite words or lines? Are there any lines that the children think they could improve?

2. Use questioning to draw out the pattern and note any features such as well-chosen words or alliteration. Avoid the temptation to tell the children. Build up a Writer's Toolkit for poetry.

Oral and practice activities

These can be slotted in at any point in the unit of work. The more children practice performing poetry, the more effective they will become.

Writing

5. You could use the 'Writer's Toolkit' or make one up in a similar vein and, with reference to the poems already read – and any others available, model the writing of poems based on the patterns used.

6. When the children can write confidently, they could try one of the long or short tasks. Once confident you can encourage children to invent their own repetitive patterns.

Where I Live

With my little eye
I can see the tall trees
by the playground railings.

With my little eye
I can see the corner shop
where we buy sweets.

With my little ear
I can hear cars whizzing
down King Street.

With my little ear
I can hear chattering shoppers
in the supermarket queues.

With my little hand
I can touch the rough bricks
on the railway bridge.

In This Room

With my little eye
I can see the whiteboard
covered with writing.

With my little eye
I can see a painting of a Pegasus
flying over the forest.

With my little ear
I can hear the heating rumble
and the sound of someone chewing
    a sweet.

With my little ear
I can hear teachers talking
but no one is listening!

With my little hand
I can touch the cold glass of milk
and feel its smooth skin.

Topsy Turvy

This morning the world
was topsy turvy.

The cars started talking
to the red buses.

The lamppost bent down
and tickled a dustbin.

The houses yawned
and fell fast asleep.

The chairs giggled
and the table sneezed.

The light began to sing
a nursery rhyme.

The floor wished
that everyone would tiptoe.

The door closed shut
and said, "Goodnight!"

Guess What I Am

I am silver and stay still,
Waiting for someone
To move into view.

If you look into me
I can swallow you up.

I am your twin
But will never know
Your name.

What am I?

Guess What I Am

I am a fly-by-night,
Silent in flight,
Scanning the fields,
Waiting to sweep by.

You might see me at rest
On a post, eyes clamped
Tight as shells –

Like a shadow
I'll come, calling
In the dark –
Who? Who? Who?

But the night
Does not answer back.
The bushes hold their breath.
The fields are locked up
So I drift by…

Till in the headlamps
You might spot me
Like a ghost of the dead
Flapping overhead…

Silly Sentences

Not last night
But the night before
24 people came knocking
at my door…

One was a postman delivering children.

One was a farmer growing cars.

One was a policeman stopping the letters.

One was a teacher teaching apples.

Animal Tongue Twisters

A lazy lion lay on the long lilo.

A tiny tiger tickled a turtle's toes.

A small snake slipped slyly to the supermarket.

Where I Live

Repeated line.

First two verses based on 'sight' sense.

Poem based on local neighbourhood.

Next two verses based on 'sound' sense.
Use real names.

Choose verbs carefully.

End on 'touch'.
Use details.

<u>With my little eye</u>
<u>I can see</u> the tall trees
by the playground railings.

With my little eye
I can see the corner shop
where we buy sweets.

With my little ear
<u>I can hear</u> cars whizzing
down <u>King Street</u>.

With my little ear
I can hear <u>chattering</u> shoppers
in the supermarket queues.

With my little hand
I can touch <u>the rough bricks</u>
on the railway bridge.

In This Room

Look for details on the classroom display.

Choose verbs with care.

A little alliteration can be effective.

Use well-chosen adjectives.

<u>With my little eye</u>
I can see the whiteboard
covered with writing.

<u>With my little eye</u>
I can see a painting of a Pegasus
flying over the forest.

With my little ear
I can hear the heating <u>rumble</u>
and the sound of someone <u>chewing</u> a sweet.

With my little ear
I can hear <u>teachers talking</u>
but no one is listening!

With my little hand
I can touch the <u>cold</u> glass of milk
and feel its <u>smooth</u> skin.

ANNOTATED VERSIONS

Topsy Turvy

This morning the world
was topsy turvy.

The cars started talking
to the red buses.

The lamppost bent down
and tickled a dustbin.

The houses yawned
and fell fast asleep.

The chairs giggled
and the table sneezed.

The light began to sing
a nursery rhyme.

The floor wished
that everyone would tiptoe.

The door closed shut
and said, "Goodnight!"

Choose everyday things that can be seen locally or in the classroom.

Bring each object alive by making it do something as if it were human. This is called personification.

Choose the verbs with care.

Try to find a way to end the poem.

Guess What I Am

I am silver and stay still,
Waiting for someone
To move into view.

If you look into me
I can swallow you up.

I am your twin
But will never know
Your name.

What am I?

Alliteration makes lines memorable.

Choose an object and list clues.

Talk as if you were the object.

End with a question.

ANNOTATED VERSIONS

Guess What I Am

Begin with 'I am…'

I am a fly-by-night,
Silent in flight,
Scanning the fields,
Waiting to sweep by.

Try addressing the reader.

Simile – using 'as'.
Simile using 'like'.

You might see me at rest
On a post, eyes clamped
Tight as shells –
Like a shadow
I'll come, calling
In the dark –

Echoes sound of owl calling.

Who? Who? Who?

But the night
Does not answer back.

Alliteration.
Choose powerful verbs.

The bushes hold their breath.
The fields are locked up

So I drift by…
Till in the headlamps
You might spot me

Simile using 'like'.

Like a ghost of the dead
Flapping over head…

14

Silly Sentences

Rhythmic opening from a playground rhyme.

Not last night
But the night before
24 people came knocking
at my door...

Silly sentences are created by swapping the nouns over.

One was a postman delivering children.

You could try swapping verbs as an alternative!

One was a farmer growing cars.

One was a policeman stopping the letters.

Animal Tongue Twisters

Make a list of animals.

A lazy lion lay on the long lilo.

Create tongue twisters by using lots of words that start with the same letter.

A tiny tiger tickled a turtle's toes.

A small snake slipped slyly to the supermarket.

ORAL ACTIVITIES

Poetry performances

There are four types of performance – whole class, group, paired and individual. The more children practise performing, the better they get. When performing there are a few key things to think about. Much of this needs to be discussed and good performance needs to be modelled by the teacher or older children. It is important to 'vary' how you say poetry – in relation to the meaning. Encourage children to think about the following points:

▶ Power – which bits need to be loud, which are soft? Whispering in a clear and dramatic voice can be very effective.

▶ Pauses – leaving a dramatic pause can also be effective.

▶ Pace – which bits should be quick (as long as they are clearly spoken) and where should you slow down?

▶ Pitch – which bits might be spoken in a high or low voice?

▶ Expression – think about the meaning and vary what is spoken – maybe harsh, angry, melancholy, joyful?

▶ Rhythm – try reading with a flowing rhythm.

Groups will need to consider how to use their voices – all together, in pairs, male/female, and so on. They will also need to consider how to stand and move – though too much movement becomes distracting. Finally, they may want to use percussive or simple musical backing.

Learning poems by heart comes quite simply through constant repetition. This will happen if you are learning a poem as a class for a poetry assembly or for a group performance. Other useful activities include:

▶ making a tape of poems for another class to listen to;

▶ making a video recording as a TV poetry performance for another class;

▶ preparing a poetry show for another class.

All these activities are invaluable as they help children internalise vocabulary and patterns of poetic language that will ultimately influence the range and quality of their own writing – and a well-known and loved poem will stay with them for the rest of their lives!

Use this poem as a model for your own writing. Look carefully at the pattern and then copy it, adding on your own ideas.

Magical Factory

In my magical factory you can make –

A dolly out of melting chocolate,

An action man out of drifting clouds,

A pen out of red flames,

A car out of magical wishes,

A fist out of bee stings,

etc.

Read the poem below and then write a similar poem yourself. To do this, follow these poetry instructions:

1 Think of a person.

2 Make a list saying what he or she is like – a colour, animal, object, place, something from nature, a feeling, a memory, a character in a book, and so on.

The Mystery Guest

She is pink as a marshmallow.

She is an earwig wriggling in a peapod.

She is the leg of a tall table.

She is the river Mersey flowing by.

She is a crisp, autumn leaf drifting down.

She is a laugh building up inside you.

She is my last birthday when I went to Gran's.

She is...

WRITER'S TOOLKIT – POETRY

When you are writing

You can:

▶ play with ideas, e.g. I saw the clouds chatting together;

▶ try to say what something is really like, e.g. raindrops look like silvery buds.

How to set your poem out

Some poems use a pattern. This might mean:

▶ a repeating line;

▶ using rhymes;

▶ verses and a chorus;

▶ a shape on the page;

▶ short and long lines.

The poet's special effects

Poets have a few special effects that they use. Think about:

▶ make sure you choose good words;

▶ chose words that do not often go together;

▶ try some alliteration;

▶ use similes with 'like';

▶ use similes with 'as... as ...'

1 Tongue Twisters

Write 4 tongue twisters. These instructions will help.

1 Select a letter to repeat (*p*).

2 Chose a subject (*a pear*).

3 Chose a word to describe it that starts with the same sound (*a prickly pear*).

4 Then say what it is doing (*a prickly pear putting*).

5 Then add on to the sentence using the same sound as much as possible (*a prickly pear putting pineapples onto a purple plate*).

1 ....

2 ....

3 ....

4 ....

2 Poetry Sentences

Complete these poetic sentences:

I can see a cat...

I can see a snake...

I can hear the wind...

I can hear the rain...

LONG TASKS

1 Secrets
Write a poem in which you make up secrets.
Use the same pattern as the poem below.

It's a secret but
my dad is superman.

It's a secret but
my dog can fly.

It's a secret but
I know a tree that can sing.

It's a secret but
I saw a cloud wave at me.

2 Special lands
Write a poem in which you make up a strange land
where anything can happen! Use the same pattern
as the poem below.

Come with me
to a land where mirrors mumble.

Come with me
to a land where taxis talk.

Come with me
to a land where bushes blush.

2 Getting going with story writing

TEACHER'S NOTES

The focus of this section is to develop the children's ability to find ideas for and plan their story writing. The strategies for planning need modelling and using as often as possible.

Story maps

Story maps show the whole of a plot visually. It can be useful to have a starting point on a map, e.g. where the main character lives. Then have a place that they are journeying to, e.g. a village. Then draw on a landscape – maybe crossing a hill, over a stream and through a forest (three places is probably sufficient or the tale may become too complex). What might happen on the way?

Storyboards

Storyboards are useful because they help to visually represent the sequence of events. Each box can be translated into a paragraph.

Story mountain

Mountains are a more abstract way of planning. However, they help to show a simple five part structure to a story, consisting of:

1. Opening
2. Build up
3. Problem
4. Resolution
5. Ending

It is useful to add relevant connectives to each section, e.g. endings might have – finally, in the end, eventually, etc.

Using flow charts

Flow charts are also handy because they help children to structure what happens, scene by scene, and leads into paragraph writing. It can be helpful to attach connectives to each box, showing how that paragraph could begin.

Connectives

When modelling writing, write connectives in red so that they stand out. These act rather like coat hangers onto which the flesh of the story hangs.

STORY MAPS

Story maps help you to see what is happening in the story.

Questions to ask yourself

Before you start drawing, think about these questions:
Where does the main character live? Where are they going?
Why are they on their journey? Who will they meet?
What will happen?

Choosing your settings

You could draw on – a cottage, a lonely tower, a palace, caves, hills, mountains, rivers, lakes, bridges, forest, a swamp.

 Writing tip

Do not have too much on the map. Keep it simple and have just three places that your character visits.

Building your characters

Main character – choose one strong main character.
Nasty character – wolf, snake, fox, magpie, troll, giant, goblin…
Helper – who helps the main character when they are in trouble?

 Writing tip

Do not have too many characters or you may get confused!
Think about what sort of character you have chosen – are they shy, bossy, brave, kind, mean? What will they say and do?

Reasons for travelling

You main character will be travelling through the story land that you have created. Where does the journey start?
Where are they going and why? Are they taking some food to someone? Taking a secret message? Visiting someone?
Going to do something – gathering firewood, going to work, looking after the sheep?

STORY PICTURE MAP

STORYBOARDS

Storyboards are a simple way of planning what will happen in your story. They look rather like a cartoon. You have to draw into the boxes the main events in your story. (You could write in the boxes). Here is an example:

Billy takes his axe and goes to find wood.

He meets a wolf.

The wolf has a thorn in its foot and Billy pulls it out.

Later on Billy is attacked by a lion.

The wolf chases it away.

Sometimes you may need more than five boxes. Remember to think about how the story will open, what happens and how it will end. Use the storyboard below to practise planning.

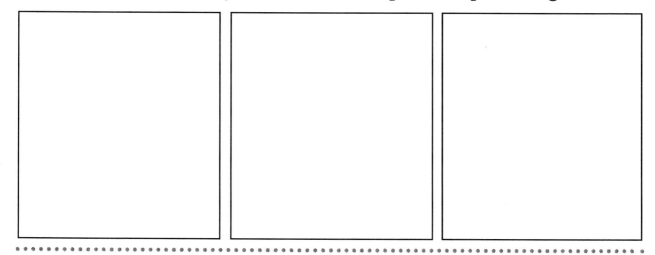

STORY MOUNTAIN

Stories are like journeys. At the beginning you send your characters off and as they are travelling through the story all sorts of things happen before they reach the end. The story mountain is a useful way to plan. It has five parts:

1 Opening

2 Build up

3 Problem

4 Resolution

5 Ending

Here is an example of a story plan using the mountain:

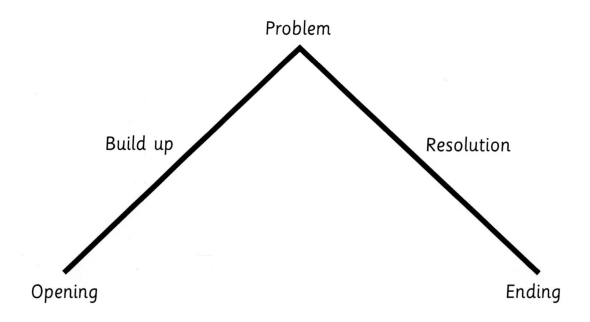

Now try drawing your own story mountain and draw or make notes on the mountain showing what happens.

STORY FLOW CHARTS

Some writers use a flow chart to show the main scenes in a story. In the example given here you can see the five main scenes – you could have many more. But be careful – the more scenes you have, then the harder it will be to write the story. It can help to keep the pattern of the story simple.

You can draw ideas or write notes onto the flow chart. Before you start writing, it can help to add on the connectives or sentence openings that start each different scene. Some people have a paragraph for each box when they write the story.

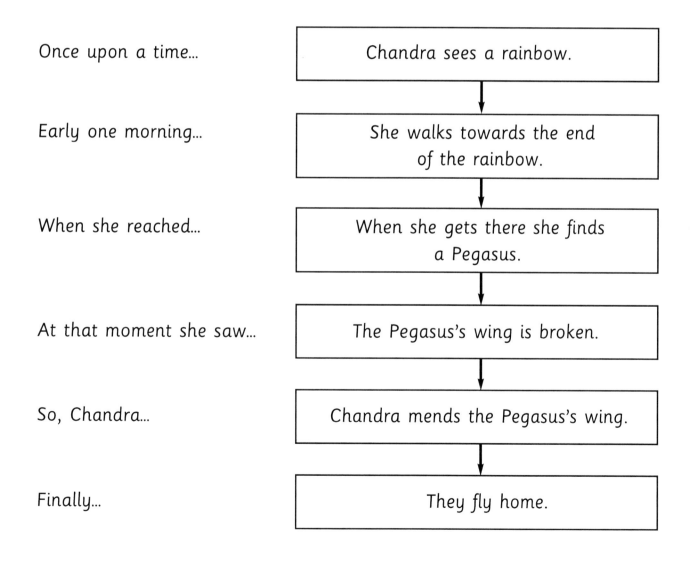

Once upon a time...

Chandra sees a rainbow.

Early one morning...

She walks towards the end of the rainbow.

When she reached...

When she gets there she finds a Pegasus.

At that moment she saw...

The Pegasus's wing is broken.

So, Chandra...

Chandra mends the Pegasus's wing.

Finally...

They fly home.

STORY CONNECTIVES

Use story connectives to link your story together. They often make good paragraph openers. Look for other useful connectives and ways to start different parts of a story. Collect these and add them to the list.

Opening connectives

Once upon a time... There once lived... Long ago there was... In a distant land... Before I was born there lived...

Build up

After... As... As soon as... Because... Before... But... During... Early one morning... First... If... Immediately... Later on... Next... One day... Or... Since... So... The next day... The next morning... Until... When... Whenever... Where... Wherever... While...

Problem

Suddenly... At that moment... Without warning...

Resolution

After... As... As soon as... Because... Before... But... During... Early one morning... First... If... Immediately... Later on... Next... One day... Or... Since... So... The next day... The next morning... Until... When... Whenever... Where... Wherever... While...

Ending

Finally... Eventually... In the end... When they reached home... So...

THE DICE GAME

How to play

1 *Finding characters*
Roll a dice to choose a good character and a baddie.
Then roll to find out how they are feeling.

2 *Sorting out settings*
Now roll the dice to find out where the story starts.
Roll again to find out where the action takes place.

3 *A key event*
Finally roll the dice to discover what may happen in the story.

4 Now draw a map, mountain, storyboard or flow chart to plan the tale.

5 You could now tell and write the story.

	Goodies	Baddies			Goodies' feelings	Baddie's feelings
1	Prince	Giant		1	Brave	Mean
2	Princess	Fox		2	Clever	Cruel
3	Farmer	Snake		3	Happy	Unkind
4	Hare	Coyote		4	Generous	Spiteful
5	Spider	Goblin		5	Sad	Jealous
6	Woodcutter	Troll		6	Lonely	Angry

THE DICE GAME

Where the story starts	Where the characters meet
1 Cottage	Cave
2 Farm	Forest
3 Market place	Old bridge
4 Palace	Lonely tower
5 Stream	Lake
6 Hut	Ruined city

What might happen?

1   Someone does something wrong.

2   Someone gets into trouble.

3   Someone wishes for something.

4   Someone is sent on a journey to get or deliver something.

5   Everything is OK until a monster/something nasty appears.

6   Something is lost or found.

7   Someone gets hurt and needs rescuing.

8   The main character finds something precious.

9   The bad character tries to steal something.

10   Someone is greedy.

Think about how the story begins, where your good character goes. Why are they going there? What happens when the baddie meets the goodie? How will it end? It can help to think of the last line first.

ORAL ACTIVITIES

1. Inventing stories

Work as a class to make stories up together. These could be just told. Try choosing ingredients (characters, settings and a key problem) and just practise turning these into a story.

2. Paired stories

Let children work in pairs to orally invent a story – or part of a story together.

3. Story circles

Put children into smallish circles to invent stories. Each child tells a section and then hands the story on.

4. Practising story sentences

Model a story sentence, e.g. 'Once upon a time there was a little girl called Daisy who lived in a cottage.' Then the children have to work in pairs coming up with their own version, e.g. 'Once upon a time there was a little goblin called Tiny who lived in a hole in a tree trunk.'

5. The objects game

Set out on a tray a range of objects. A child selects three objects. Children then have to work out a story involving the three objects. If this is going to be hard, start with one – and then build it up.

6. Retelling well-known tales

Select a well-known tale and practise retelling it. Let children retell tales that they know from previous years, e.g. 'Three Little Pigs', 'Goldilocks', etc.

7. Telling rhymes as stories

Make a list of well-known nursery and traditional rhymes. Many of these tell a short tale. Take one and retell it as a story, e.g. *'Humpty was feeling miserable. He mooched around the place all day long till his Mum said, "Go down to the corner shop and get some tea. But whatever you do, do not play around on the town wall..."*

1. Practise planning

Begin planning by using story maps as these are the most visual and concrete. Then move on to storyboards and mountains. End the year with flow charts. It is worth spending time regularly just making stories up and quickly mapping them onto a story mountain planner. Demonstrate how to do this and then involve the children. Get them using whiteboards to plan ideas.

2. Tell the plans

Demonstrate how to turn the plans into stories. On some occasions the teacher does this – but also the children should be involved.

3. Map rhymes and known tales

Take well-known stories and nursery rhymes. Map these onto a story mountain. Of course, you may need more than one mountain peak. Indeed if a story has lots of action then you may need a range of mountain peaks! Start with something simple like Cinderella.

4. List problems

Try to encourage children not to have too many dilemmas in their plans because this makes the writing of the story difficult. The best advice is to keep it simple. Make lists of possible problems or dilemmas. Raiding picture books for ideas can be helpful.

5. Collecting names

Have a class collection of good names for characters and settings.

6. Change known tales

Take a story that everyone knows well and then rewrite it but make changes to it. There are different ways you could alter a known tale, e.g.

▶ change the characters;

▶ change the setting;

▶ modernise it;

▶ alter the ending dramatically;

▶ add in more events or take events out.

Story ideas

Choose an idea and think about it for several days before you write the story.

1 The teacher draws a monster on the board that comes alive.

2 There is a noise at the back of where you live and you find a dragon.

3 The main character wakes up and has changed into someone else – a teacher, a parent, a cat, a dog.

4 A child wakes up with a superpower – flying, strength, x-ray eyes...

5 The main character finds a magic ring.

6 The main character enters another world through – a door, window, trap door, mirror.

7 Two children find a wishing machine.

8 Two children shrink and fall through the floorboards.

9 A child finds an invisibility cloak.

10 A parcel arrives containing something mysterious.

11 Supposing you could... fly!

12 What if... a tree could talk!

13 A father boasts that his child can turn wool into gold.

14 The main character meets a talking animal, e.g. an owl.

3 Traditional tales

TEACHER'S NOTES

The focus of this section is to develop the children's ability to create their own fairy stories. It is helpful if they have read many traditional tales and have got to know some quite well. These could be acted out, turned into zig-zag books or learned and told to a younger class.

Reading as a writer

1. Read and discuss 'Jack and the Hare'. Ask children to draw three boxes around the beginning, middle and end. Discuss what happens in each section. Note that 'Jack and the Hare' and 'Mary and the Owl' have a simple three-part structure – beginning, middle and end. However, 'Jack and the Wolf' and 'Mary and the Turnips' have a five part structure – opening, build up, problem/exciting event, resolution, ending - and this is reflected in the use of paragraphs.

2. Use questioning to draw out different features. Circle any words or phrases that might be useful, especially connectives. Avoid the temptation to tell the children. Build up a Writer's Toolkit for traditional tales.

Oral and practice activities

These can be slotted in at any point in the unit of work. It is best to do short but frequent practice. This encourages speed of thought.

3. Use some of the oral activities to practise story telling. The more the children make up and play with stories, the more likely they are to internalise the patterns of language that they will need in order to write their own.

4. Use the practice activities to support the grammar needed – especially a fluidity with sentence construction and combination. Practise on mini-whiteboards so that the children get skilful at joining sentences together.

Writing

5. The teacher should now use the 'Writer's Toolkit' and, with reference to the examples already read – and any others available, model the writing of a fairy tale.

6. When the children can write confidently, they could try one of the long or short tasks.

Jack and the Hare

Once upon a time there was a boy called Jack who lived in a village. One day he was down by the river fishing when he heard a funny noise. It was a squeaking and squealing sound coming from behind a bush. Jack crept round and there he found a hare that had been caught in a metal trap. The trap had sharp teeth like a mouth and it was biting on the hare's leg.

So Jack knelt down and freed the hare. It bounded away and soon had disappeared. Jack went back to his fishing. A while later he slipped into the river by accident and the river began to drag him away from the bank. Now Jack couldn't swim so he was in great danger. He called for help but he was so far away from his village that no one could possibly hear him. Poor Jack drifted on down the river. He swept under bridges and past rocky islands, all the time going further and further away from his home.

In the end, just as Jack thought that he would never get back onto dry land again, he saw the hare pushing a branch into the water. It stuck right out and as he drifted past, Jack leaned out and grabbed the end of the branch. Then the hare began to pull him in. He pulled and he pulled and all the while Jack was getting closer and closer to the bank. At last, Jack was on the bank, thanking his new friend, the hare. They lit a fire to dry Jack's clothes and the hare ran home to fetch a little kettle and a tiny loaf of bread. Soon they were having tea and toast, with a bramble marmalade. So that is how Jack met his best friend – the hare.

Mary and the Owl

Once upon a time there was a girl called Mary who lived in a tree house. One night she was trying to get to sleep when an owl flew up to see her. It was a white barn owl and at first it gave Mary a terrible fright. She thought that it was a ghost flying around. But when she had calmed down she saw that it was only a little barn owl. The owl stood on a branch outside her window and winked its amber eyes at her. Every time Mary turned back to go to sleep the owl tapped on the window until in the end Mary realised that the owl wanted Mary to follow her.

So Mary climbed down to the ground and followed the owl. It flew along the forest paths like a white shadow flickering ahead of her. It led her deeper and deeper into the woods until they came to a cave. From inside the cave Mary could hear the sound of voices. It was two men talking. They had built a fire and were having their evening meal. Mary could hear them discussing how they were going to capture the birds and mammals that lived in the forest and sell them to a zoo.

In the end Mary crept away and ran back through the forest to the village. She knocked on the door of the first cottage that she came to and told the people living there about the two men. Soon the villagers had gathered together and they decided to chase the men away. Mary was worried because she had seen that the men had guns but she had an idea. An hour later the foxes from the forest sat outside the cave and howled. The men ran outside to see what was making such a noise. Then the owls swooped down like ghosts in the night. The men were so frightened that they began to run into the trees. Then the foxes and the dogs chased them, barking and biting at their heels until they had run right away. Luckily, they were never seen again!

Jack and the Wolf

Once upon a time there lived a boy called Jack. Early one frosty morning he was out walking in the forest looking for firewood. He picked up all the sticks that had fallen from the trees and he made a large pile. He carefully put the sticks into a sack and began to drag them back home.

Now, he hadn't travelled very far when he heard behind him the sound of feet, pitter-pattering through the forest. Somebody or something was following him. At first he saw nothing but then he noticed the long, grey shape of a wolf. Poor Jack dropped the sack and ran as fast as he could but it was no good. The wolf soon caught up with him. It stood on the path and stared at him. It had sharp white teeth and bright red eyes. Poor Jack's knobbly knees shook so much that he could hardly stand still.

Suddenly, much to Jack's amazement, the wolf lay down and whined. It held out its paw. Jack could see that the wolf's paw was swollen. It had a thorn stuck in it. So Jack crept forwards and gently tugged the thorn out. The wolf licked his face as if to thank Jack.

After that Jack made his way back home. When he got there his Mum wanted to know where the firewood had gone. Jack told her his story but she did not believe that he had helped a wolf. Why, all the wolves in the forest were wild creatures and surely would have eaten him up for their supper.

From that day on, he always had a friend and companion. Whenever he went travelling through the forest, the wolf would follow him like a shadow slipping between the trees.

Mary and the Turnips

Once upon a time there was a greedy miller who had a daughter called Mary. Every morning the miller made Mary go out of the mill, down the lane and into their next-door neighbour's field to steal turnips. It was silly really because neither of them liked turnips and they were fed up with eating turnip soup so often!

Now, one cold morning when the sun was hardly up, Mary made her way down the lane, over the stile and into the turnip field. She was stuffing turnips into a sack when she was sure that one of them spoke. "Put me back where I belong," said a tiny voice. Mary was most surprised because she was sure that a turnip had spoken to her. Then she looked closer and she saw that it was not a turnip at all. She had grabbed hold of a teeny tiny person by the scruff of the hair instead of a turnip. The teeny tiny person looked very cross.

Suddenly, the teeny tiny person started shouting and yelling and the next thing that Mary knew all the turnips in the field seemed to get up out of the ground and began to run towards her. Yes – she was in a field of teeny tiny people and they all seemed very cross!

So Mary dropped the teeny tiny person and ran over the field, jumped across the style and ran back up the lane to the old windmill where she lived with her father. She sat down on a sack of corn, puffing and panting, and told him what had happened.

After that she never ever went stealing from the turnip field and her father was far too scared to do it himself! So, they never had to have turnip soup again.

ANNOTATED VERSION – MODEL 1

Jack and the Hare

Opening connective.
Useful connective to start the action.
Alliteration.
Powerful verb.
Metaphor/simile to show how nasty the trap is.
Useful connective to lead into the next piece of action.

More well-chosen verbs that help to build the picture, showing what is happening.

Useful connective to indicate that the end of the tale is beginning.
Powerful verbs.
Note repetition of 'pulled' and 'closer' – a typical traditional tale device.

Typical ending line, 'so that is how…'

<u>Once upon a time</u> there was a boy called Jack who lived in a village. <u>One day</u> he was down by the river fishing when he heard a funny noise. It was a <u>squeaking</u> and <u>squealing sound</u> coming from behind a bush. Jack <u>crept</u> round and there he found a hare that had been caught in a metal trap. <u>The trap had sharp teeth like a mouth</u> and it was biting on the hare's leg.

<u>So</u> Jack knelt down and freed the hare. It bounded away and soon had disappeared. Jack went back to his fishing. A while later he <u>slipped</u> into the river by accident and the river began to <u>drag</u> him away from the bank. Now Jack couldn't swim so he was in great danger. He called for help but he was so far away from his village that no one could possibly hear him. Poor Jack <u>drifted</u> on down the river. He <u>swept</u> under bridges and past rocky islands, all the time going further and further away from his home.

<u>In the end</u>, just as Jack thought that he would never get back onto dry land again, he saw the hare pushing a branch into the water. It stuck right out and as he <u>drifted</u> past, Jack leaned out and <u>grabbed</u> the end of the branch. Then the hare began to pull him in. <u>He pulled and he pulled and all the while Jack was getting closer and closer to the bank.</u> At last, Jack was on the bank, thanking his new friend, the hare. They lit a fire to dry Jack's clothes and the hare ran home to fetch a little kettle and a tiny loaf of bread. Soon they were having tea and toast, with a bramble marmalade. <u>So that is how Jack met his best friend – the hare.</u>

Beginning – introduce main character, setting and use 'one day' to start the action – a creature is trapped.

Middle – main character rescues the trapped creature, demonstrating a kind action. But then the main character gets into a dangerous situation.

Ending – main character is rescued by the creature – who is repaying the kindness that has been shown. They become friends.

39

ANNOTATED VERSION – DEMONSTRATION 1

Mary and the Owl

Use of opening connective and same sentence structure as 'Jack and the Hare' for opening sentence (using 'who lived…' to establish setting. Use interesting descriptive words. Choose powerful verbs.

Useful connective to introduce the next part of the story.
Simile – using 'like'.

Useful connective to begin the last part of the story.

Useful connective to introduce the next part.

Connective.

Powerful verb and simile to help build the description so the reader can imagine what is happening.
Alliteration.
Typical ending.

Once upon a time there was a girl called Mary who lived in a tree house. One night she was trying to get to sleep when an owl flew up to see her. It was a white barn owl and at first it gave Mary a terrible fright. She thought that it was a ghost flying around. But when she had calmed down she saw that it was only a little barn owl. The owl stood on a branch outside her window and winked its amber eyes at her. Every time Mary turned back to go to sleep the owl tapped on the window until in the end Mary realised that the owl wanted Mary to follow her.

So Mary climbed down to the ground and followed the owl. It flew along the forest paths like a white shadow flickering ahead of her. It led her deeper and deeper into the woods until they came to a cave. From inside the cave Mary could hear the sound of voices. It was two men talking. They had built a fire and were having their evening meal. Mary could hear them discussing how they were going to capture the birds and mammals that lived in the forest and sell them to a zoo.

In the end Mary crept away and ran back through the forest to the village. She knocked on the door of the first cottage that she came to and told the people living there about the two men. Soon the villagers had gathered together and they decided to chase the men away. Mary was worried because she had seen that the men had guns but she had an idea. An hour later the foxes from the forest sat outside the cave and howled. The men ran outside to see what was making such a noise. Then the owls swooped down like ghosts in the night. The men were so frightened that they began to run into the trees. Then the foxes and the dogs chased them, barking and biting at their heels until they had run right away. Luckily, they were never seen again!

Beginning – introduce main character, setting and use 'one night' to start the action – a creature demands to be followed.

Middle – creature leads main character to a different place where they overhear 'baddies' planning to do something wrong.

Ending – main character manages to chase off the 'baddies' by getting help from others.

40

Jack and the Wolf

Traditional tale opening. Useful connective to get story going. Traditional activity.

Underlined: Once upon a time there lived a boy called Jack. Early one frosty morning he was out walking in the forest looking for firewood. He picked up all the sticks that had fallen from the trees and he made a large pile. He carefully put the sticks into a sack and began to drag them back home.

Opening that introduces main character and setting, then gets the story going. Main character is doing something ordinary.

Typical story-telling voice. Build up suspense by not mentioning immediately the creature – use a sound or vague shape.

Now, he hadn't travelled very far when he heard behind him the sound of feet, pitter pattering through the forest. Somebody or something was following him. At first he saw nothing but then he noticed the long, grey shape of a wolf. Poor Jack dropped the sack and ran as fast as he could but it was no good. The wolf soon caught up with him. It stood on the path and stared at him. It had sharp white teeth and bright red eyes. Poor Jack's knobbly knees shook so much that he could hardly stand still.

Build up – the story really starts – the main character meets a creature that is frightening – could be a shark, an ogre, a ghost, a lion!

Notice descriptive detail to help reader imagine what is happening.

Useful connective to introduce 'problem' or exciting event. Notice use of adverb – collect and list several to use.

Suddenly, much to Jack's amazement, the wolf lay down and whined. It held out its paw. Jack could see that the wolf's paw was swollen. It had a thorn stuck in it. So Jack crept forwards and gently tugged the thorn out. The wolf licked his face as if to thank Jack.

The problem – in this case the wolf has a thorn in its foot. It could be that the ferocious animal is in some way in need of help/rescue.

Useful connective to introduce resolution phase.

After that Jack made his way back home. When he got there his Mum wanted to know where the firewood had gone. Jack told her his story but she did not believe that he had helped a wolf. Why, all the wolves in the forest were wild creatures and surely would have eaten him up for their supper?

Resolution – the problem is solved and the main character begins to wind up the story. In this case the main character helps the creature.

Typical use of a question in a traditional tale.

Typical way of introducing end of tale. Simile to build the picture.

From that day on, he always had a friend and companion. Whenever he went travelling through the forest the wolf would follow him like a shadow slipping between the trees.

Ending – showing how the main character has changed as a result of what has happened. In this case main character makes friend with creature.

Mary and the Turnips

Typical opening connective for a traditional tale.

Note how miler is described – collect other such useful words – selfish, cruel, mean, etc.

Jack and Mary are typical traditional tale names.

Useful connective to get story going.

Note sentence in which three things happen.

Use details.

Connective to introduce 'problem' part of story.

Note repetition from end of previous paragraph.

Use of 'so' to introduce resolution phase of story.

Note use of three things happening in each sentence.

Use of connective for 'ending' phase of story.

Typical final line.

<u>Once upon a time</u> there was a <u>greedy</u> miller who had a daughter called Mary. Every morning the miller made Mary go out of the mill, down the lane and into their next door neighbour's field to steal turnips. It was silly really because neither of them liked turnips and they were fed up with eating turnip soup so often!

<u>Now, one cold morning</u> when the sun was hardly up, <u>Mary made her way down the lane, over the stile and into the turnip field</u>. She was stuffing turnips into a sack when she was sure that one of them spoke. "Put me back where I belong," said a tiny voice. Mary was most surprised because she was sure that a turnip had spoken to her. Then she looked closer and she saw that it was not a turnip at all. She had grabbed hold of a teeny tiny person by the <u>scruff of the hair</u> instead of a turnip. The teeny tiny person looked very cross.

<u>Suddenly,</u> the teeny tiny person started shouting and yelling and the next thing that Mary knew all the turnips in the field seemed to get up out of the ground and began to run towards her. Yes – she was in a field of teeny tiny people and <u>they all seemed very cross!</u>

<u>So</u> Mary dropped the teeny tiny person and ran over the field, jumped across the style and ran back up the lane to the old windmill where she lived with her father. She sat down on a sack of corn, puffing and panting, and told him what had happened.

<u>After that</u> she never ever went stealing from the turnip field and her father was far too scared to do it himself! <u>So, they never had to have turnip soup again.</u>

Opening – introduces main characters – has main character doing something that they should not be doing.

Build up – the story gets going - main character is doing whatever they are not supposed to be doing – and something surprising happens.

Problem – something awful, problematic, difficult, exciting, dreadful... happens.

Resolution – main character sorts out the problem – in this case by escaping.

Ending – shows what the main character has learned from the events.

ORAL ACTIVITIES

1. Retelling known tales

Select a fairly simple story such as 'The Billy Goat's Gruff'. Read a version to the class. Draw a picture map of the story and let the children draw their own. Demonstrate how to use the picture map to help retell the tale. It can help to write key sentence openers, connectives or repetitive phrases onto the map. Put the children into pairs to tell and retell the story. Try whole class retellings. It can help to put actions to specific parts of the tale as this makes them more memorable.

2. Innovating on known tales

Once the children know the story well enough to retell it without stumbling then they could try changing the story to make it their own. They could:

▶ Change characters – make a good character bad!

▶ Change the setting.

▶ Change the opening/ending.

▶ Retell it from another view, e.g. retelling the 'Three Little Pigs' from the wolf's viewpoint!

▶ Change events or the dialogue.

▶ Change the style of telling, e.g. modernise 'Snow White'.

They could also be encouraged to add to the tale:

▶ Add in new incidents, especially if they fit the pattern.

▶ Build up description.

▶ Include more dialogue.

▶ Add in a moral at the end.

▶ Bring in new characters.

3. Inventing your own

Bring in a selection of objects. A child has to select three objects and then everyone invents a tale, using those objects. This could begin with drawing a story map and then telling in pairs.

1. Sentences from words

This game could be played orally or by using mini-whiteboards. The advantage of using mini-whiteboards is that you will be able to check for the basics of sentence construction = meaning plus use of capital letter and full stop.

Provide a word, e.g. 'dog', and the children have to make up a sentence using that word. Keep on at the stage of providing just one word till everyone is remembering to punctuate accurately. Then 'promote' the class and move on to 2 and ultimately, 3 words, e.g. jelly, shark, because.

This game is excellent for simply practising sentence construction and gaining the automatic habit of demarcation. You can move on to two or three sentences. When selecting words you can provide words that might well come into a traditional tale, e.g. wolf, cottage, miller, etc.

2. Boring sentences

This game is helpful because it provides an opportunity for children to look carefully at the quality of vocabulary and how this influences meaning. Provide a dull sentence (the cat went along the wall) and the children have to make it more interesting. They might want to:

▶ Change words to intensify their meaning, e.g. The Siamese sneaked along the wall.

▶ Add in words (the fat cat went along the rough wall) or drop in a phrase (the thin and cruel cat went along the wall) or clause (the cat, which was weary, went along the wall).

▶ Add on more words at either end (after breakfast was finished, the cat went along the wall, because it was still hungry).

▶ Reorder the words (along the wall went the cat).

3. Changing sentences

Provide a sentence and ask the children to change it. Give instructions for changing. You could ask them to:

► turn it into a question;

► turn it into an exclamation;

► add in a simile;

► add in some alliteration;

► add in two adjectives;

► add in an adverb;

► make it shorter;

► make it longer;

► change the tense;

► make it say the opposite;

► make the character sound angry;

► rewrite it as if it was in a newspaper report.

4. Using connectives

Provide a traditional story connective and the children have to complete the sentence.

Once, not twice, but once upon a time there lived...

Early one frosty morning...

Long ago, in a distant land, there lived...

A long time ago there was...

When the world was just begun...

WRITER'S TOOLKIT – TRADITIONAL TALES

1 Organise the story into a clear beginning, middle and end. A more developed story will have two or three short paragraphs in the middle.

2 Try to get a simple pattern into your story. Sometimes having things happening in threes can be useful. Often there will be a journey, a warning, a wish to be granted or an evil character to overcome. Drawing a simple story map is a good way to plan.

3 Plan endings where good triumphs over evil, a lesson has been learned and everyone lives happily ever after.

4 Use typical characters – *king, queen, princess, farmer, woodcutter, old woman, miller, beggar, hare, spider, tortoise, fox, wolf…*

You may need a good main character and a bad character. Bad characters may well be greedy, cruel or selfish. The main character is sometimes the third son or daughter and will be kind. This kindness will be repaid.

5 Choose typical settings, e.g. forest, pond, paths, tower, castle, market, cave, ocean, burrow…

6 Use objects typical of this type of story – *a spinning wheel, a magic purse, a singing sack, a mirror that talks, a porridge pot, an axe, a pot of gold, a comb, a handkerchief, a house on chicken legs.*

7 Use connectives that are typical of this type of story, such as – *once upon a time, one day, so, suddenly, after that, in the end.*

SHORT TASKS

1 Write the opening part of a story about a princess who could not laugh and a poor boy who tries to cheer her up. Use only the space provided below.

....

....

....

....

....

....

....

....

....

....

2 Look at these first two pictures from a storyboard. Write the first two paragraphs that might accompany the pictures.

LONG TASKS

1 Write a story about a boy who rescues a bird that has been trapped in a bush. The bird grants him three wishes – what happens?

2 Write a story about a greedy king who finds a magic object and keeps it for himself. He could find:
- a purse that always has gold;
- a pot that always provides food;
- a magic tablecloth;
- a sack that can trap anything;
- a purse that if you put in one, you can take out two;
- a mirror that tells the truth;
- an apple of life;
- or something of your own choosing.

3 Write a story about a girl or boy who is warned not to go into the forest.

4 Write a story about a boy or girl who makes friends with a creature.

4 Stories with familiar settings

TEACHER'S NOTES

The focus of this section is to develop the children's ability to write a simple story with a familiar setting. Children will be at different stages and, therefore, both three- and five-part stories are included to read and to demonstrate, and teachers must decide which is more appropriate. It would be possible to begin with the simple three-part and introduce the five-part later in the year.

Reading as a writer

1. Read and discuss either 'The Birthday Present' or 'The Shopping Trip'. Ask children how the story is structured. A summary of each section could be fitted into one of the planning diagrams, such as the flow chart on page 27.

2. Use questioning to draw out different features related to starts, endings and variety in sentences. Avoid the temptation to tell the children. Build up a Writer's Toolkit for stories with familiar settings.

Oral and practice activities

These can be slotted in at any point in the unit of work. It is best to do short but frequent practice. This encourages speed of thought.

3. Use some of the oral activities to practise story planning. It is important that children talk through ideas as much as possible before they start to write.

4. Use the practice activities to support the grammar needed in story writing.

Writing

5. The teacher should now use the 'Writer's Toolkit' and, with reference to the example(s) already read, model the writing of a short story with a familiar setting. This will work best if done in stages and set against the children's planning. The teacher can model a start and then write it. The children will then use their plan to do the same. A three-part and a five-part story is included for demonstration, followed by annotated versions.

6. When the children can write confidently, they could try one of the long or short tasks.

The Birthday Present

Danny was very excited. It was his birthday and he was seven years old. First thing in the morning he rushed into his parents' bedroom.

"Wow!" he shouted when he saw the pile of presents.

"Happy birthday, Danny," his Mum and Dad said, smiling.

His baby sister cooed and gurgled but Danny was sure she was trying to join in. He had some Lego and the game he wanted but the best present was the one from Uncle Jim. He couldn't wait to show his friends so he carefully packed the box into his school bag.

When Danny got to school, his teacher had already put his name on the board and lit the birthday candles. He unpacked the bag and carried the box to the front. All his friends were watching. The box was silver and shiny and had pictures of machines all over it. Danny opened the lid and reached inside. There was nothing there!

"Oh no!" he cried. "I've lost Uncle Jim's present!"

"How can you have done that?" Mrs Watson asked. "Did you drop anything on the way to school?"

"I don't think so," Danny sobbed. "Maybe it's in the cloakroom." He looked and looked between the coats hanging on the pegs but he couldn't find his birthday present. It *was* lost!

Danny did not enjoy his birthday at school. He kept thinking about what Mum and Dad and Uncle Jim would say. They would be cross.

At last it was time to go home. He put the empty box in his bag with his lunchbox and his reading folder and walked slowly outside to meet Mum. When he saw her, he could not believe his eyes. She was holding Robotman high in the air.

"You left him on the table!" Mum shouted.

Danny's friends rushed over and they all agreed that Robotman was the most brilliant present ever.

Spiders!

Class 2C were learning about spiders. Billy loved it. There were lots of pictures of spiders around the room with labels to show you the names of the different parts. When Miss Cox said that some spiders are dangerous, Katie Benton started to cry.

"I hate spiders!" she said.

"We haven't got any spiders in here, Katie," Miss Cox said.

After dinner, everyone was busy drawing pictures of spiders and writing about them. They were going to make a class book. Suddenly, Katie screamed.

"Ahh! There's a spider on the desk!" Everyone rushed over and saw a big, hairy spider scuttle over the edge of the desk, down the leg and off into the corner.

"That's Webby, my pet spider," Billy said. "He's got out! I brought him because of the spider topic. Be careful! Someone might squash him!"

Everyone looked around. At last Katie spotted Webby inside the unifix cube tray.

"I think we've scared him," she said. She grabbed a measuring container and popped it over the spider. Billy slipped a piece of paper under it. Webby was safe.

"Thanks, Katie," Billy said. "You caught my spider. I thought you were scared."

"I forgot about it with all the excitement," Katie said. She enjoyed the topic as much as Billy after that. The next day she wrote a story about capturing a huge spider and Miss Cox gave her a gold star.

The Shopping Trip

It was Saturday. Mum and Carrie were shopping in town. Crowds of people pushed along the pavements and Carrie was getting bored and very tired.

"I need to go into Benton's," said Mum. "I want to buy some new towels. It will be very busy so make sure you stay close to me and don't wander off."

Carrie sighed. They walked past the make-up counters and got in the lift to the second floor. Mum let go of Carrie's hand and began to sort through piles of soft towels. At last she decided on four big green towels and four smaller cream ones. They walked to the check-out but there was a long line. They waited.

After a few minutes, Mum noticed her friend nearby and they started chatting. The queue moved slowly. Carrie was fed up. She looked around, spotted the toy department across the shop and decided to go and look while Mum was talking.

Carrie found a mountain of soft toys and tried to decide which she would like for her next birthday. Next she looked at a display of bright pink Barbie bits and pieces. She thought she liked the castle that lit up but it did look expensive.

After a while, Carrie remembered Mum. She ran back to the till but Mum wasn't there. Carrie was filled with panic. Suddenly a voice filled the shop: "Would Carrie Stevens please go to the information desk where her mother is waiting."

When Carrie got there, she found her Mum holding two big bags of towels and looking very worried.

"Where did you go?" Mum shouted. "I told you not to wander off."

"I went to look at the toys," Carrie explained. "You were talking to Mrs Box."

"I should have watched you," Mum said, "but you must remember to stay close in busy shops."

On the way home, Carrie told Mum what she had seen in the toy department and what she wanted for her birthday!

Bramble's Short Adventure

One Saturday afternoon, Sam and his older brother Tim set out for the park with Bramble, their dog.

It was a sunny day and a lot of people were out enjoying themselves. Tim pushed Sam on the swings and chased him up and down the climbing frame. Next they played a game of football on the grass. This was hard because Bramble got in the way and bounded around their legs. They got so hot that Tim bought ice-creams and they sat on the grass to eat them.

After that, the two boys went down to the stream and threw some bread to the ducks. A mother duck led her family of tiny, yellow ducklings up the bank on the other side and waddled away. Bramble barked, leapt into the water and swam across after them.

"Stop, Bramble!" Tim shouted.

Another dog appeared on the other side and Bramble stopped chasing the ducks and rushed after it.

"Come back, you silly dog!" Sam yelled.

By the time the boys had crossed the stream by the stone bridge, Bramble was out of sight. They did not know what to do. They searched all around the park. They searched up and down the High Street. But they couldn't find him.

"Mum will be so cross!" Sam cried.

At last the boys decided to go home because it was nearly time for tea. As they walked up the road, they could see Mum waiting for them. Next to her was Bramble!

"Bramble!" Sam shouted. "You're not lost!"

"He came back by himself about half an hour ago," Mum said. "He must have wanted his tea early!"

ANNOTATED VERSION – MODEL 1

The Birthday Present

Danny was very excited. It was his birthday and he was seven years old. First[1] thing in the morning he rushed into his parents' bedroom.

"Wow!" he shouted[2] when he saw the pile of presents.

"Happy birthday, Danny," his Mum and Dad said, smiling.

His baby sister cooed[2] and gurgled but Danny was sure she was trying to join in. He had some Lego and the game he wanted but the best present was the one from Uncle Jim. He couldn't wait to show his friends so he carefully packed the box into his school bag.

When[1] Danny got to school, his teacher had already put his name on the board and lit the birthday candles. He unpacked the bag and carried the box to the front. All his friends were watching. The box was silver and shiny and had pictures of machines all over it. Danny opened the lid and reached inside. There was nothing there!

"Oh no!" he cried[2]. "I've lost Uncle Jim's present!"

"How can you have done that? Mrs Watson asked. "Did you drop anything on the way to school?"

"I don't think so," Danny sobbed[2]. "Maybe it's in the cloakroom." He looked and looked between the coats hanging on the pegs but he couldn't find his birthday present. It *was* lost!

Danny did not enjoy his birthday at school. He kept thinking about what Mum and Dad and Uncle Jim would say. They would be cross.

At last[1] it was time to go home. He put the empty box in his bag with his lunchbox and his reading folder and walked slowly outside to meet Mum. When[1] he saw her, he could not believe his eyes. She was holding Robotman high in the air.

"You left him on the table!" Mum shouted.

Danny's friends rushed over and they all agreed that Robotman was the most brilliant present ever.

STORY START – Danny's birthday. Who, where, when. Information about the main character.

Information about the presents.

Reader knows that the present from Uncle Jim is very important but does not know what it is.

STORY END – Mum has the toy. He had left it at home. Link back to the beginning.

Reader finds out what the toy is.

Sadness followed by excitement.

Key:
[1] Time connectives to move the story on.

[2] Words instead of said so that the reader knows how the character is feeling.

MIDDLE – Danny at school – thinks he has lost present.

School setting.

Cloakroom described to help the reader imagine the setting.

54

Spiders!

Class 2C were learning about spiders. Billy loved it. There were lots of pictures of spiders around the room with labels to show you the names of the different parts. When Miss Cox said that some spiders are dangerous, Katie Benton started to cry[2].

"I hate spiders!" she said.

"We haven't got any spiders in here, Katie," Miss Cox said.

After[1] dinner, everyone was busy drawing pictures of spiders and writing about them. They were going to make a class book. Suddenly, Katie screamed[2].

"Ahh! There's a spider on the desk!" Everyone rushed over and saw a big, hairy spider scuttle over the edge of the desk, down the leg and off into the corner.

"That's Webby, my pet spider," Billy said. "He's got out! I brought him because of the spider topic. Be careful! Someone might squash him!"

Everyone looked around. At last[1] Katie spotted Webby inside the unifix cube tray.

"I think we've scared him," she said. She grabbed a measuring container and popped it over the spider. Billy slipped a piece of paper under it. Webby was safe.

"Thanks, Katie," Billy said. "You caught my spider. I thought you were scared."

"I forgot about it with all the excitement," Katie said. She enjoyed the topic as much as Billy after that. The next day[1] she wrote a story about capturing a huge spider and Miss Cox gave her a gold star.

ANNOTATED VERSION – MODEL 2

The Shopping Trip

1. START –
Carrie and Mum go
shopping. Carrie
warned to stay
close.
Who, where, when
and why.

It was Saturday. Mum and Carrie were shopping in town. Crowds of people pushed along the pavements and Carrie was getting bored and very tired[2].

"I need to go into Benton's" said Mum. "I want to buy some new towels. It will be very busy so make sure you stay close to me and don't wander off."

Detail of the time and place. Shop has a name.

2. Carrie bored.
Mum is busy.
Carrie wanders off.

Detail about the
inside of the shop
and about what
Mum is buying.

Carrie sighed[2]. They walked past the make-up counters[3] and got in the lift[3] to the second floor. Mum let go of Carrie's hand and began to sort through piles of soft towels. At last[1] she decided on four big green towels and four smaller cream ones. They walked to the check-out[3] but there was a long line. They waited.

After a few minutes[1], Mum noticed her friend nearby and they started chatting. The queue[3] moved slowly. Carrie was fed up[2]. She looked around, spotted the toy department[3] across the shop and decided to go and look while Mum was talking.

Key:
[1] Time connectives to move the story on.

[2] Tells the reader something about the character.

[3] Words related to shops.

3. Carrie spends
time in the toy
department.

Details of toys.

Carrie found a mountain of soft toys and tried to decide which she would like for her next birthday. Next[1] she looked at a display of bright pink Barbie bits and pieces. She thought she liked the castle that lit up but it did look expensive.

4. Carrie goes back
– but Mum is not
there.

After a while[1], Carrie remembered Mum. She ran back to the till but Mum wasn't there. Carrie was filled with panic[2]. Suddenly a voice filled the shop: "Would Carrie Stevens please go to the information desk[3] where her mother is waiting."

5. END - Finds
Mum – reminds
her to stay close –
link to the start.

When[1] Carrie got there, she found her Mum holding two big bags of towels and looking very worried[2].

"Where did you go?" Mum shouted[2]. "I told you not to wander off."

"I went to look at the toys," Carrie explained. "You were talking to Mrs Box."

"I should have watched you," Mum said, "but you must remember to stay close in busy shops."

On the way home[1], Carrie told Mum what she had seen in the toy department and what she wanted for her birthday.

Bramble's Short Adventure

1. START –
Boys and dog
go to park.

One Saturday afternoon[1], Sam and his older brother Tim set out for the park with Bramble, their dog.

Characters given names.
Who, where and when.

2. They have
fun in the
park.
Detail of
weather to add
to setting.

It was a sunny day and a lot of people were out enjoying themselves. Tim pushed Sam on the swings and chased him up and down the climbing frame. Next[1] they played a game of football on the grass. This was hard because Bramble got in the way and bounded around their legs. They got so hot[2] that Tim bought ice-creams and they sat on the grass to eat them.

Lots of words related to a playground in the park. Lots of action to show that the boys are enjoying themselves.

3. Dog chases
ducks and
then another
dog. Runs off.

Another
setting in the
park.

After that[1], the two boys went down to the stream and threw some bread to the ducks. A mother duck led her family of tiny, yellow ducklings up the bank on the other side and waddled away. Bramble barked, leapt into the water and swam across after them.
"Stop, Bramble!" Tim shouted[2].
Another dog appeared on the other side and Bramble stopped chasing the ducks and rushed after it.
"Come back, you silly dog!" Sam yelled[2].

4. Boys look
for dog but
can't find him.

By the time[1] the boys had crossed the stream by the stone bridge, Bramble was out of sight. They did not know what to do. They searched all around the park. They searched up and down the High Street. But they couldn't find him.
"Mum will be so cross![2]" Sam cried.

Detail of setting added.

5. END – Dog
went home by
himself.

Surprising end.

At last[1] the boys decided to go home because it was nearly time for tea. As they walked up the road, they could see Mum waiting for them. Next to her was Bramble!
"Bramble!" Sam shouted[2]. "You're not lost!"
"He came back by himself about half an hour ago," Mum said. "He must have wanted his tea early!"

Key:
[1] Time connectives to move the story on.

[2] Tells the reader more about how the characters feel.

ORAL ACTIVITIES

Planning games

Let the children have practice planning simple three- and five-part stories with familiar settings.

1. Give the children a start and then continue to tell the story as a class or a group.

2. Use pieces of coloured card (3 or 5 of them) to represent the parts of the story. Fix them to the board. Scribe their story ideas as they come up with them. Demonstrate writing down the main idea, in note form, behind each part of the story.

3. Make sets of cards which give simple plot outlines – see planning chapter. Let the children expand these out loud by giving the characters names and by developing a familiar setting.

Alternative endings

Re-read the stories up to the final section. Talk about other ways the story might end.

Talk about the way that the original stories have a link back to the start.

<table>
<tr><td>Sam and Tim went to the park.</td><td>They played in the park.</td></tr>
<tr><td>They got hot so they had an ice-cream.</td><td>They fed the ducks.</td></tr>
</table>

Time connectives

Work in groups to collect as many time connectives as possible. Work on whiteboards to write different sentences beginning with a time connective.

Sequencing a story

Make sets of statements covering the main points of a story. The cards opposite and below are examples that can be copied and cut out.

Mix up the cards and ask the children to quickly sequence the events. Let them experiment with different time connectives at the start of each sentence.

Writing in the past tense

Re-write a section from one of the stories in the present tense and ask the children to correct it. This could be done as a class on an OHT or by pairs working on paper. Another idea is to leave out certain verbs and let the children search for alternatives.

Bramble chased the ducks.	**The boys could not find Bramble.**
They went home.	**Bramble was already at home.**

Familiar settings

Use these pictures to brainstorm ideas to describe familiar settings. Work in pairs with whiteboards to put the ideas into sentences.

WRITER'S TOOLKIT

1 Organise the story into a clear beginning, middle and end. A more developed story will have two or three short paragraphs in the middle. E.g. 'The Shopping Trip' and 'Bramble's Short Adventure'.

2 Use stock ideas of warnings, losing things, being lost, being found, etc.

3 Plan endings that link back to the beginning (*Mum reminds Carrie that she had warned her not to wander off*) or which have a twist to surprise the reader (*the dog was not lost – it had gone home*).

4 Give the characters names and let the reader know something about them.

5 Choose settings that are well known to make it easier to describe.

▶ *…looked and looked between the coats hanging on the hooks.*

▶ *There were lots of pictures of spiders around the room and labels to show the names of the different bits.*

▶ *They walked past the make-up counters and got into the lift to the second floor.*

▶ *Tim pushed Sam on the swings and chased him up and down the climbing frame.*

6 Use time connectives – *next, later, a few minutes after that, at last.*

SHORT TASKS

1 Write the start of a story set on this beach.

2 Write the start of a story set in this bedroom.

LONG TASKS

1 Use these pictures to write a "forgotten" story.

1

2

3

2 Use this plan to write a "warning" story.

Jack's friend comes

Warning to boys – Keep off flower beds

Football on grass

Ball on flowers – damage

Boys sort it out

HOW WILL YOUR STORY END?

TEACHER'S NOTES

The focus of this section is to develop the children's ability to write a simple story with a magical theme or an adventure. Children will be at different stages and, therefore, both three- and five-part stories are included to read and to demonstrate and teachers must decide which is more appropriate. It would be possible to begin with the simple three-part and introduce the five-part later in the year.

Reading as a writer

1. Read and discuss either 'The Magic Dust' or 'The Move'. Ask children how the story is structured. A summary of each section could be fitted into one of the planning diagrams, such as the flow chart on page 27.

2. Use questioning to draw out different features related to starts, endings and variety in sentences. Avoid the temptation to tell the children. Build up a Writer's Toolkit for stories with magical or adventurous events.

Oral and practice activities

These can be slotted in at any point in the unit of work. It is best to do short but frequent practice. This encourages speed of thought.

3. Use some of the oral activities to practise story planning. It is important that children talk through ideas as much as possible before they start to write.

4. Use the practice activities to support the grammar needed in story writing.

Writing

5. The teacher should now use the 'Writer's Toolkit' and, with reference to the example(s) already read, model the writing of a short story containing magic or adventure. This will work best if done in stages and set against the children's planning. The teacher can model a start and then write it. The children will then use their plan to do the same. A three-part and a five-part story is included for demonstration, followed by annotated versions.

6. When the children can write confidently, they could try one of the long or short tasks. The children can use the boxes on page 78 to plan three- or five-part stories before they start to write.

The Magic Dust

Lizzie couldn't sleep. She lay in bed and tossed and turned. She had read her school reading book to her Mum and her Mum had read to her. Now she was in bed but she just wasn't tired. She wanted to be outside playing like her older brother and sister. Suddenly, something caught her eye. A bright light sparkled and shone on the window sill. The light moved up and down and at last came to a stop on top of Lizzie's piggy bank. Lizzie jumped out of bed and tip-toed towards it. She was amazed! There, sitting with its legs crossed and holding a tiny pot in its hand, was a tiny pixie.

Before Lizzie could open   pixie spoke.
"Here, take thi·   ver you and see what happens!"

Lizzie d·   hat the pixie ordered.
Streams of st·   v filled the room and lifted Lizzie rig   d the room she flew.
The pixie flew ·

"I'm going ·   ·d the window, it opened for her! S·   ·e air, high over the garden, high over   ·ne pixie flickered brightly beside her ·

[handwritten annotations: "photocopy", "this highlights something happened", "magical", "adventure"]

At last, Lizzie be·   ·jeel tired. She yawned. The pixie pointed to show the way home and it wasn't long before they were back in Lizzie's bedroom. The pixie waved his hand and in a swirl of silver sparks Lizzie landed on her bed.

"Goodnight!" she called. The pixie smiled. Lizzie could still see the magic dust sparkling all around him.

"Keep it a secret and we'll do the same tomorrow," the pixie said.

Lizzie did keep it a secret and she didn't tell her Mum where the coloured bits on the carpet came from.

A Very Special Paint Box

Uncle Mark gave Timmy a paint box and brush for his seventh birthday.

"It's not an ordinary paint box, though," Uncle Mark said so only Timmy could hear. "You'll see."

Timmy didn't see but he had no time to try it out that day. He didn't get it out the next day either, or the one after that, because he had so many new toys and games.

A week later, Timmy was inside. It was raining hard and he was feeling bored. Suddenly, he remembered the paint box and rushed over to the desk. He decided to paint a picture for Uncle Mark and get Mum to send it in the post.

As he picked up the brush, a very strange thing happened. The handle glowed and felt warm in his fingers. Timmy moved the brush towards the paint. Before he even touched it, a rainbow of colours leapt up and covered the bristles.

"Wow!" shouted Timmy. "I'll paint a robot."

He brushed the paper and could not believe his eyes. The moment the paint touched the paper, a little robot walked stiffly off the paper and onto the floor. Timmy wasn't bored any more that afternoon. He painted some soldiers, a puzzle and a lorry and he played with them all. As the paint dried, they slowly vanished, back into the paper they had come from.

At five o'clock, Timmy's Mum poked her head round the door.

"Time for tea," she said. "Oh, I'm glad you're using Uncle Mark's present. What have you painted?"

Timmy looked at the blank paper. "Well, nothing exactly," he said. He knew his Mum wouldn't understand. "I'll have another go tomorrow."

The Move

One morning, Fergus Fieldmouse and his family were woken up by a tremendous rumbling. It was coming from the far side of their peaceful field on the edge of Mr Smith's farm. Fergus and his wife Maisie peered outside.

"Oh no!" cried Fergus. "Mr Smith is going to use this field. Look! He's cutting down the hedge and digging everything up."

"We have to move at once!" Maisie Fieldmouse said. "The machine will be at this end of the field soon."

It was a very busy day. The two oldest children helped their Mum and Dad pack everything they had. Little Billy Fieldmouse did not understand what was happening and kept getting in the way. At last they were ready. Fergus loaded the bags onto a sort of sledge so that they could drag it along. They curled up together on the ground and tried to sleep but they kept thinking about the machines.

Next morning, the little family set out before it was even daylight. They had to cross the open field and reach the land on the other side. They would look for a new home there.

"Oh, what if we don't get there before it's dark!" cried Maisie. "It's such a long way!"

Fergus led them around the edge of the field. They were in the shade of the hedge and they could let Billy rest without being spotted by a fox or a crow.

However, by the middle of the afternoon, Fergus knew that they would not get to safety unless they took another route. Billy was so tired now that he was asleep on top of the bundles. Fergus looked around.

"We'll have to go across," he said.

He led the way between the long grasses. Every few minutes they stopped to listen. Suddenly, the roar of a machine got louder. It was coming their way. Fergus pulled with all his might. Maisie and the older children pushed from behind. The sledge sped between the grasses and the machine passed them with only a tiny space to spare.

The gap into the next field was close now. They had to get there before the machine turned round. A bird swooped down low but did not see them.

"Just keep going," Fergus said. "We can do it!" They plodded on. The grass was shorter and the sledge was easier to pull. They came to the gap, pulled the sledge through and sat down puffing on the other side. They were safe!

Fergus and Maisie found another little home and lived there happily for years, far away from Mr Smith's machines.

A Forest Adventure

Bip was a tiny elf who lived on the edge of Blackberry Forest with his family. His brother, Seb, was ill and his Mum was getting worried.

"I don't know why these herbs haven't worked!" she cried. "You must go into the forest and find the Wise One and ask her what to do."

Bip liked the forest and often played there with his friends. He skipped along and sang as he went. Soon he crossed the gurgling stream using the magic stones and started out on the path through the dark trees. Silvey, his glow worm friend, came along to light his way.

He had been walking for about half an hour when something grabbed him from behind.

"Where are you going?" Mean Mob said. Oh no! Just his luck! Mean Mob was with his gang. They tied him to a tree and ran off laughing.

Bip started to cry. His Mum was waiting for him and Seb was ill. What was he going to do? He tried shouting but no-one heard.

He had almost given up hope when he heard voices.

"Help!" he shouted. "Over here!" It was Lex and Tex, his friends from school.

"What are you doing?" they asked.

"Mob got me," Bip said sadly. "I have to go and see the Wise One. Seb is ill."

Tex untied him and they all went on together. The trees were very close together in that part of the forest and Silvey glowed brightly to show them the narrow path.

The Wise One sat on a huge toadstool outside her front door. She nodded as they told her about Seb and handed Bip a bottle full of a green, bubbly mixture.

"Take this home," she said. "This will make him well."

The little elves set out at once. They followed Silvey along the narrow path, back over the stones and soon came out of the forest. Bip's Mum was standing at her door. She looked worried.

"Where have you been?" she asked. "You've been a long time. I was worried."

Bip did not tell his Mum about his adventure but he did tell the truth.

"I met Lex and Tex," he said. "Here's the mixture. The Wise One said Seb will be better very soon."

She was right. Seb was soon out of bed, running around and annoying everybody as usual!

The Magic Dust

Key:
[1] Time connectives to move story forward.

[2] Words related to light and colour – to build up image of magic.

New character – pixie.

MIDDLE – Lizzie and pixie fly off into the night.

Magic in the story to enable Lizzie to fly.

Deliberate repetition.

STORY START – Lizzie can't sleep – bright light – pixie appears. Ordinary setting in her house. Character named – reader knows she isn't tired. Description – magical happenings.

Lizzie couldn't sleep. She lay in bed and tossed and turned. She had read her school reading book to her Mum and her Mum had read to her. Now[1] she was in bed but she just wasn't tired. She wanted to be outside playing like her older brother and sister. Suddenly, something caught her eye. A bright light sparkled and shone[2] on the window sill. The light moved up and down and at last[1] came to a stop on top of Lizzie's piggy bank. Lizzie jumped out of bed and tip-toed towards it. She was amazed! There, sitting with its legs crossed and holding a tiny pot in its hand, was a tiny pixie.

Before Lizzie could open her mouth, the pixie spoke.
"Here, take this," he said. "Shake it all over you and see what happens!"
Lizzie didn't even think about it. She did what the pixie ordered. Streams of stars in all the colours of the rainbow[2] filled the room and lifted Lizzie right up into the air. Round and round the room she flew. The pixie flew with her.
"I'm going out!" Lizzie called. When[1] she reached the window, it opened for her! She found herself soaring through the air, high over the garden, high over the street, high over the town. The pixie flickered brightly[2] beside her all the way.

More magic to get Lizzie back to bed.

Magical description.

END – Lizzie back home – promise of another adventure.

Coloured bits on carpet – so it really happened.

At last[1], Lizzie began to feel tired. She yawned. The pixie pointed to show the way home and it wasn't long[1] before they were back in Lizzie's bedroom. The pixie waved his hand and in a swirl of silver sparks[2] Lizzie landed on her bed.
"Goodnight!" she called. The pixie smiled. Lizzie could still see the magic dust sparkling[2] all around him.
"Keep it a secret and we'll do the same tomorrow," the pixie said.
Lizzie did keep it a secret and she didn't tell her Mum where the coloured bits on the carpet came from.

A Very Special Paint Box

Uncle Mark gave Timmy a paint box and brush for his seventh birthday.

"It's not an ordinary paint box, though," Uncle Mark said so only Timmy could hear. "You'll see."

Timmy didn't see but he had no time to try it out that day. He didn't get it out the next day either, or the one after that, because he had so many new toys and games.

A week later[1], Timmy was inside. It was raining hard and he was feeling bored. Suddenly, he remembered the paint box and rushed over to the desk. He decided to paint a picture for Uncle Mark and get Mum to send it in the post.

As he picked up the brush, a very strange thing happened. The handle glowed and felt warm in his fingers. Timmy moved the brush towards the paint. Before he even touched it, a rainbow of colours leapt up and covered the bristles.

"Wow!" shouted Timmy. "I'll paint a robot."

He brushed the paper and could not believe his eyes. The moment the paint touched the paper, a little robot walked stiffly off the paper and onto the floor. Timmy wasn't bored any more that afternoon. He painted some soldiers, a puzzle and a lorry and he played with them all. As the paint dried[1], they slowly vanished, back into the paper they had come from.

At five o'clock[1], Timmy's Mum poked her head round the door.

"Time for tea," she said. "Oh, I'm glad you're using Uncle Mark's present. What have you painted?"

Timmy looked at the blank paper. "Well, nothing exactly," he said. He knew his Mum wouldn't understand. "I'll have another go tomorrow."

Key:
[1] Time connectives to move the story forward.

START –
Timmy has a new paint box. He's told it's not ordinary – this sets up a magical event.

Timmy busy. Time passing – "that day", "next day", "the one after that".

Carefully chosen phrases – "glowed", "warm", "rainbow of colours leapt up".

Timmy bored – decides to use the paint box.

MIDDLE –
Paint brush is magic – when he paints, the picture becomes real.

Carefully chosen – "walked stiffly".

Magic.

More magic.

END –
Nothing on paper – doesn't tell about magic.

The promise of more magic tomorrow because Timmy is going to use the paint set again.

ANNOTATED VERSION – MODEL 2

The Move

1. START – family needs to move.

Characters and setting are introduced.

Reason for the move.

One morning[1], Fergus Fieldmouse and his family were woken up by a tremendous rumbling[2]. It was coming from the far side of their peaceful field on the edge of Mr Smith's farm. Fergus and his wife Maisie peered outside.

"Oh no!" cried Fergus. "Mr Smith is going to use this field. Look! He's cutting down the hedge and digging everything up."

"We have to move at once!" Maisie Fieldmouse said. "The machine will be at this end of the field soon."

It was a very busy day. The two oldest children helped their Mum and Dad pack everything they had. Little Billy Fieldmouse did not understand what was happening and kept getting in the way. At last[1] they were ready. Fergus loaded the bags onto a sort of sledge so that they could drag it along. They curled[2] up together on the ground and tried to sleep but they kept thinking about the machines.

3. Set out on dangerous journey.

Maisie's speech tells the reader she is worried.

Billy needs rest – more danger for others.

Next morning[1], the little family set out before it was even daylight. They had to cross the open field and reach the land on the other side. They would look for a new home there.

"Oh, what if we don't get there before it's dark!" cried Maisie. "It's such a long way!"

Fergus led them around the edge of the field. They were in the shade of the hedge and they could let Billy rest without being spotted by a fox or a crow.

However, by the middle of the afternoon[1], Fergus knew that they would not get to safety unless they took another route. Billy was so tired now that he was asleep on top of the bundles. Fergus looked around.

"We'll have to go across," he said.

He led the way between the long grasses. Every few minutes[1] they stopped to listen. Suddenly, the roar[2] of a machine got louder. It was coming their way. Fergus pulled with all his might. Maisie and the older children pushed from behind. The sledge sped[2] between the grasses and the machine passed them with only a tiny space to spare.

5. END – They reach safety.

Still in danger until the very last minute.

Link to a happy home at the beginning of the story.

The gap into the next field was close now. They had to get there before the machine turned round. A bird swooped[2] down low but did not see them.

"Just keep going," Fergus said. "We can do it!" They plodded[2] on. The grass was shorter and the sledge was easier to pull. They came to the gap, pulled the sledge through and sat down puffing[2] on the other side. They were safe!

Fergus and Maisie found another little home and lived there happily for years, far away from Mr Smith's machines.

Key:
[1] Time connectives to move the story forward.

[2] Carefully chosen words.

2. Pack for the move.
Detail to build up the idea of a lot going on.
Billy – too young to understand.

4. Problems on the way.

Danger building up.

"Suddenly" introduces the danger.
Machine only just missed them.

Key:
1 Time connectives to move story forward.

2 Carefully chosen words and phrases.

1. START –
Bip must go into the forest. Fantasy characters and setting introduced.

A Forest Adventure

Bip was a tiny elf who lived on the edge of Blackberry Forest with his family. His brother, Seb, was ill and his Mum was getting worried.

"I don't know why these herbs haven't worked!" she cried. "You must go into the forest and find the Wise One and ask her what to do."

Bip liked the forest and often played there with his friends. He skipped[2] along and sang as he went. Soon[1] he crossed the gurgling[2] stream using the magic stones and started out on the path through the dark trees. Silvey, his glow worm friend, came along to light his way.

2. Journeys through forest.

Magic mentioned – fantasy setting.

3. Problem – gets grabbed.

He had been walking for about half an hour[1] when something grabbed[2] him from behind.

"Where are you going?" Mean Mob said. Oh no! Just his luck! Mean Mob was with his gang. They tied him to a tree and ran off laughing.

Bip started to cry. His Mum was waiting for him and Seb was ill. What was he going to do? He tried shouting but no-one heard.

He had almost given up hope when he heard voices.

"Help!" he shouted. "Over here!" It was Lex and Tex, his friends from school.

"What are you doing?" they asked.

"Mob got me," Bip said sadly. "I have to go and see the Wise One. Seb is ill."

Tex untied him and they all went on together. The trees were very close together in that part of the forest and Silvey glowed brightly[2] to show them the narrow path.

4. Friends save him.

Still got problems – scary forest.

5. END –
Get medicine and go home. Brother OK.
Fantasy setting – "sat on a huge toadstool".
Wise One not named – doesn't need a name - "nodded" – shows understanding.

Everything back to normal.

The Wise One sat on a huge toadstool outside her front door. She nodded as they told her about Seb and handed Bip a bottle full of a green, bubbly mixture[2].

"Take this home," she said. "This will make him well."

The little elves set out at once. They followed Silvey along the narrow path, back over the stones and soon came out of the forest. Bip's Mum was standing at her door. She looked worried.

"Where have you been?" she asked. "You've been a long time. I was worried."

Bip did not tell his Mum about his adventure but he did tell the truth.

"I met Lex and Tex," he said. "Here's the mixture. The Wise One said Seb will be better very soon."

She was right. Seb was soon out of bed, running around and annoying everybody as usual!

ORAL ACTIVITIES

1. Statements and questions

Put question words on coloured card on the board – **Who? What? Where? When? Why?**

Create statements based on the stories they have read. The children listen carefully and use one of the words on the board to turn it into a question. Make up a **sound** and an **action** for a question mark. E.g.

Fergus and Maisie heard a noise.
What did Fergus and Maisie hear?

The paint brush glowed.
Why did the paint brush glow?

As well as practising the skill of writing questions, this will also develop simple oral comprehension.

2. Characters in stories

Talk about the characters in the stories you have read. What do we know about them. Brainstorm words to describe:

▶ Lizzie

▶ Timmy

▶ Fergus

▶ Bip

Think about how they might look. As an extension, the children could draw and label pictures of the characters. They could also brainstorm using characters in other stories they have read.

1. Sentence Doctor – to continue to develop the idea of a sentence.

Give the children a number of non-sentences based on a story they have just read.

They should work in pairs to correct. They should first mark where the mistake is and could then write in their books or on whiteboards for the activity.

E.g.   Lizzie lay bed and tossed and turned.
A bright light on the window sill.
Lizzie out of bed and tiptoed towards it.

There will be lots of different ways that the children can complete the sentence.

2. A setting

Discuss with the children the different parts of the picture that could be described.

► Light/dark among trees

► Day/night

► Animals & birds

► Sounds

► Path

Children should work in pairs on whiteboards to write a short description of the wood.

3. Expanding sentences

Use the same question words on cards. **How** could be included.

Give the children a simple sentence. It can be based on one of the stories or on a well-known nursery rhyme. Explain that they are going to play a game and they may have to make up detail that was not in the story or rhyme. They pick a card and then try to answer the question. In some cases, it may be impossible. You could make it more fun by keeping a score.

E.g. *Timmy started to paint.*

Why? Timmy started to paint because he was bored.

Where? Timmy started to paint on a large piece of paper.

How? Timmy started to paint very carefully.

4. Drop in game

Once again, start with a series of simple sentences. This time they could be on card. A noun should be written in a different colour.

The children then "drop in" an adjective to describe the noun. Keep going with the same sentence and see how many different words they come up with.

Make sure that you also play this game on whiteboards to give them practice at writing it correctly.

5. Story telling

Tell magic and adventure stories around the class as described in the section on stories with familiar settings.

WRITER'S TOOLKIT – ADVENTURE

1 Write an opening that includes a setting and introduces characters.

2 Give characters names and tell the reader something about them. Use human or animal characters and make them contrasting, good and bad. Use dialogue.

3 Think of a series of events that builds up – use stock ideas of journeys, being lost or chased, or events at night.

4 A simple adventure will have a beginning, middle and end. A more developed story needs a complication and a climax ('The Move' and 'A Forest Adventure').

5 A resolution which may link back to the start.

6 Write in the past tense with time connectives: *later that morning, very early next day.*

7 Connectives to introduce suspense – *suddenly, without warning.*

8 Use of adverbs, adjectives, similes, expressive verbs, etc.

 # WRITER'S TOOLKIT – MAGICAL

A magical story could be an adventure but in addition:

▶ story must include something involving magic, e.g. *wishes that come true, magical objects that move on their own, characters that appear or disappear, magic wands or cauldrons,* etc.

SHORT TASKS   **1 A character**

Give this character a name. Write a paragraph to show what she is like.

2 A setting

Write a description of the setting in this picture.

LONG TASKS

1 Write a story called THE MAGIC KEY.

2 Write a story called RABBIT'S GARDEN ADVENTURE.

Use these boxes to plan your idea before you write.

6 Recounts

TEACHER'S NOTES

The focus of this section is to develop the children's ability to write simple recounts. This is included because although it is not mentioned in the NLS framework, it is a form of writing that might appear in the SATs and it is a form of writing that should not be neglected for a whole year! The one thing that children do know about and that matters to them is their own life and so writing recounts should be a key source for talking and writing.

Reading as a writer

1. Read and discuss 'Visiting the Budgies'. Ask children how the writing is structured. Draw their attention to the opening which includes – when, who, where and what.

2. Use questioning to draw out different features especially the consistent use of past tense, the use of particular names (Aunty, Hastings) and especially note the use of time connectives to start paragraphs and link ideas within paragraphs. Underlining these in colour can be helpful visually. Avoid the temptation to tell the children. Build up a Writer's Toolkit for recounts.

Oral and practice activities

These can be slotted in at any point in the unit of work. It is best to do short but frequent practice. This encourages speed of thought.

3. Use some of the oral activities to practise recounting incidents from their own lives. They could also talk in role as a character from a story or from an incident in history. It is important that children have the opportunity to talk the text type before writing.

4. Use the practice activities to support the grammar needed in recount writing.

Writing

5. The teacher should now use the 'Writer's Toolkit' and, with reference to the example already read – and any others available, model the writing of a recount. This will work best if related to an activity the children have done – a class trip or an incident from a story. To assist with planning, either retell the events, draw the sequence in a storyboard or use a timeline.

6. When the children can write confidently, they could try one of the long or short tasks.

Visiting the Budgies

At the weekend Mum and I went to visit my great Aunt in Hastings.

When we arrived, it was still morning. She was waiting for us. Soon we were upstairs in her little flat.

First she gave Mum a cup of tea so that she could rest after the long car journey.

Then Aunty took me into her little room and showed me her budgies. She has five of them in silvery cages. They perch on little swings and look at themselves in their little mirrors. They chatter away so that there is quite a lot of noise.

While we were there, Aunty got out some birdseed and I was allowed to feed the budgies. My favourite is a green and yellow budgie called Charlie. He is very tame and Aunty let me take him out of his cage. He sat on my finger and talked to me. He did not try to fly away. Aunty told me that the other budgies were naughty. If she gets them out of the cage, they fly straight off and hide on the curtain rail.

At lunch time we took Aunty into Hastings and had a meal in a café by the seafront. We could see the waves crashing on the promenade. It was quite a stormy day.

Once we had finished eating we walked along the promenade and sometimes the waves nearly made us wet. It was very exciting.

Later on we drove Aunty back to her budgies and then made our way back home. It had been a very exciting day. When I am older I want to keep budgies.

Jack Climbs High

This morning I had the most amazing adventure.

Early in the morning I woke up and was amazed to see that there was an enormous beanstalk growing outside my window. Those beans that the little old man gave me in exchange for Gertie must have been magic beans after all!

First I leaped out of bed. I dashed outside and looked up. The beanstalk was so tall that it seemed to have grown higher than the clouds.

So, I began to climb. I climbed for three hours. I climbed straight through the clouds and just above them I found myself in another land.

While I was there I saw a road leading to a giant's castle. I crept in through the kitchen door. The giant's wife told me that he would be coming home soon so she hid me inside the oven.

When the giant came into the kitchen he roared and shouted, "Fee, fi, fo thumb, I smell the blood of an Englishman. Be he alive or be he dead. I'll grind his bones to make my bread!" I was so frightened that I kept shaking.

Later on he fell asleep so I crept out from my hiding place. I stole some of his money and ran out of the kitchen and back to the beanstalk. I climbed down as fast as I could.

Finally, I reached the bottom. You should have seen my Mum's eyes when she heard where I had been and saw the gold! It was an exciting adventure and when I feel brave again, I am going to go back to the giant's castle because he has a goose there that lays golden eggs.

ANNOTATED VERSION – MODEL 1

Use of temporal connectives to show the passing of time and to help sequence events.

Make sure that it is written in the past tense.

Use well-chosen words to build up the picture for the reader.

Try to include interesting detail or mention things that people say.

Use specific names of people and places as this is about something real that has happened.

Try to summarise by commenting on what you thought about the event.

Visiting the Budgies

At the weekend Mum and I went to visit my great Aunt in Hastings.

When we arrived, it was still morning. She was waiting for us. Soon we were upstairs in her little flat.

First she gave Mum a cup of tea so that she could rest after the long car journey.

Then Aunty took me into her little room and showed me her budgies. She has five of them in silvery cages. They perch on little swings and look at themselves in their little mirrors. They chatter away so that there is quite a lot of noise.

While we were there, Aunty got out some birdseed and I was allowed to feed the budgies. My favourite is a green and yellow budgie called Charlie. He is very tame and Aunty let me take him out of his cage. He sat on my finger and talked to me. He did not try to fly away. Aunty told me that the other budgies were naughty. If she gets them out of the cage, they fly straight off and hide on the curtain rail.

At lunch time we took Aunty into Hastings and had a meal in a café by the seafront. We could see the waves crashing on the promenade. It was quite a stormy day.

Once we had finished eating we walked along the promenade and sometimes the waves nearly made us wet. It was very exciting.

Later on we drove Aunty back to her budgies and then made our way back home. It had been a very exciting day. When I am older I want to keep budgies.

Opening – when, who, what and where – recount based on a real incident.

Establish what happened first.

Interesting incident.

Add in extra interesting detail.

What happened in the middle of the day.

Adding a further exciting incident.

Final paragraph – comment made about how the author 'felt' plus a look to the future.

Jack Climbs High

Use of temporal connectives to show the passing of time and to help sequence events.

<u>This morning</u> I had the most amazing adventure.

Opening – when, who, what.

<u>Early in the morning</u> I woke up and was amazed to see that there was an enormous beanstalk growing outside my window. Those beans that the little old man gave me in exchange for Gertie must have been magic beans after all!

Set the scene. (A recount based on a well-known fairy tale – the writer takes the role of a character.)

Make sure that it is written in the past tense.

<u>First</u> I <u>leaped</u> out of bed. I <u>dashed</u> outside and looked up. The beanstalk was so tall that it seemed to have grown higher than the clouds.

The first incident.

Use detail to help paint the events for the reader.

<u>So</u>, I began to climb. I climbed for three hours. I climbed straight through the clouds and just above them I found myself in another land.

What happened next.

<u>While</u> I was there I saw a road leading to a giant's castle. I crept in through the kitchen door. The giant's wife told me that he would be coming home soon so she hid me inside the oven.

Main incidents.

<u>When</u> the giant came into the kitchen he roared and shouted, "Fee, fi, fo thumb, I smell the blood of an Englishman. Be he alive or be he dead. I'll grind his bones to make my bread!" I was so frightened that I kept shaking.

Use of detail to make recount interesting, e.g. quoting what someone says.

Keep to the past tense.

<u>Later on</u> he fell asleep so I crept out from my hiding place. I <u>stole</u> some of his money and ran out of the kitchen and back to the beanstalk. I climbed down as fast as I could.

Describe other people's reactions to events.

<u>Finally,</u> I reached the bottom. <u>You should have seen my Mum's eyes</u> when she heard where I had been and saw the gold! <u>It was an exciting adventure</u> and when I feel brave again, <u>I am going to go back to the giant's castle because he has a goose there that lays golden eggs</u>.

What happened in the end.

Comment on the events.

A look to the future.

ORAL ACTIVITIES

1. News

One of the best sources for recount writing is children's own experiences. Most classes have some sort of time for 'news'. This can be carried out orally with children working in pairs, telling their partner about what happened at the weekend. You could ask children to tell you who has just told them about something interesting or exciting that has happened. This encourages and values listening.

Move pairs around so that the news has to be retold – this provides an opportunity for oral redrafting – refining what is said. You could model this in front of the children. Ultimately, some children could stand up and tell their news to the class. Encourage the use of time connectives.

2. Show and tell

Many classes no longer seem to have time for 'show and tell' but children all the way through primary school enjoy this activity. It is best carried out at a fixed time each week. Children are encouraged to take turns. They bring something in to trigger a talk. This can be about a holiday, a pet, a hobby and so on. More sophisticated forms of 'show and tell' also invite children to tell stories, perform poems, sing or carry out short sketches.

3. Anecdotes

Many rich sessions can come out of telling anecdotes. It is best to lead this by telling some anecdotes yourself. These might well be based around key themes such as:

▶ places – secret places, special places, favourite places, places that are scary…

▶ events – holidays, family gatherings, celebrations, worst times, sad times, happy times, funny incidents, arguments, a time I was in trouble…

▶ people – unusual relatives, memorable people, scary people, old friends, first friends, grans and grandads…

4. Hot seating

Children take it in turns to be in role as a character from a traditional tale or the class story. They are questioned by the others about their motives, what has happened and what they intend to do next.

1 Sentence completion

These parts of sentences are all from recounts. Complete them.

Yesterday our class...

Last week I...

After that we...

After lunch we...

Later on we...

Early the next morning...

Finally...

2 Sentence copycat

Look carefully at these sentences and copy them by repeating the part that is written in italic. The first is done for you, to show how it is done.

On Tuesday morning our class sang in assembly.

On Tuesday morning our class spent three hours building a rocket.

When we reached the pier my Dad bought an ice cream.

The first thing we did was to go on 'Oblivion' which is the best ride.

Immediately, I ran back to where I thought the others were standing.

Everyone felt that *it had been the best school trip ever.*

3 Correct it

Read these sentences and correct them. There is at least one mistake in each sentence.

I slipped down the hillside and rolls other and other.

Standing in frunt of me wos an enormouse dog.

My Mum took a foto of me and my sister togever.

Me and Tina had a grate time larst weekend when we flies to Paris.

Gran gave us backed beens for tee and let us wotch televijun.

4 Join

Use a connective to join the pairs of sentences together. The first is done for you. There is a list of connectives to help.

The van stopped. We jumped out.

As the van stopped, we jumped out.

The dog ran up to us. We stood still.

We rang the front door bell. The door flew open.

We stopped by the giraffes. A small boy started to cry.

The zookeeper threw fish. The seals started to bark!

My bike hit a stone. I tumbled to the ground.

| as | as soon as | after | before | immediately | while |
| when | whenever | although | so | because | but |

WRITER'S TOOLKIT – RECOUNT

Planning

To help you plan a recount you could:

► retell what happened, just to help you sort out the events in the right order;

► draw a storyboard to show the main events in order;

► draw a timeline and jot on the main events.

The opening

To write the opening paragraph you need to think about –

► When – did this happen?

► Who – was there?

► Where – did it happen?

► What – were you there for?

For instance:
Last weekend our family went to Bristol Zoo to see the new panda.

The middle

Now write the events in order. You might find it best to give a paragraph to each main event. Choose things that others would find interesting. Use plenty of descriptive detail. Use time connectives to introduce what happened, e.g. *first, next, after that, then, later on, at lunch, when, while, so, in the afternoon, finally, at the end of the day, that evening…*

The ending

In your last paragraph comment on what you felt about what happened. For instance:
It was a great trip and I think that all my friends would love to go there as well.

SHORT TASKS

1 Write a short recount about what you did at playtime.
Start with the words 'At playtime I...'

2 Write a short recount about coming to school this morning.
Start with the words, 'This morning I...'

3 Make up a short recount about a playtime in your school in which a unicorn is found.

4 Make up a short recount about coming to school in a spaceship.

LONG TASKS

1 Pretend that you are Jack and write a letter to a friend telling them about what happened to you when you climbed the beanstalk to steal the goose that lays golden eggs.

2 Pretend that you are Cinderella and write a letter to a friend telling them about how you managed to get to the ball.

3 All of us have been in trouble at some time in our lives. Think about a time that you got into trouble at home or in school. What did you do? What happened? How did you feel? Write a recount titled '*A time I got into trouble*'.

4 Here is a list of subjects that you could write a recount about. Choose one that you think others will be interested in.

- an argument
- a time I did something disobedient
- breaking a warning
- a funny event
- my best holiday
- a sad time
- visiting a relative
- the wedding
- the disaster
- moving school
- making a new friend
- my first day at school
- how I found my best friend
- what I like to do best at weekends
- a special time
- a long journey
- staying in a hotel
- when we went camping
- flying in a plane
- going on a ferry
- a visit to the city
- a visit to the countryside

Instructions

TEACHER'S NOTES

The focus of this section is to develop the children's ability to write simple instructions. It is important to introduce a practical element into this unit. The children should both *do* something and then write instructions as well as write instructions and then try to *carry them out*.

Reading as a writer

1. Read and discuss 'How to make beans on toast for supper'. Ask children how the writing is structured. Look at the use of the title, side headings and numbered points starting on different lines.

2. Use questioning to draw out different features related to use of "bossy verbs" and impersonal tone. Avoid the temptation to tell the children. Build up a Writer's Toolkit for instructions.

Oral and practice activities

These can be slotted in at any point in the unit of work. It is best to do short but frequent practice. This encourages speed of thought.

3. Use some of the oral activities to practise giving clear instructions. It is important that children talk through ideas as much as possible before they start to write.

4. Use the practice activities to support the grammar needed in instructional writing.

Writing

5. The teacher should now use the 'Writer's Toolkit' and, with reference to the example already read – and any others available, model the writing of a set of instructions. This will work best if related to an activity the children have done. The idea for making a puppet could be substituted for something the class is working on.

6. When the children can write confidently, they could try one of the long or short tasks. It would be a good idea if they grew the seeds on the window sill before attempting the related assessment task.

How to make a puppet

WHAT YOU NEED

- a piece of felt
- pins
- marker pens
- large needle and coloured thread
- ribbons, buttons and wool for decoration
- scissors

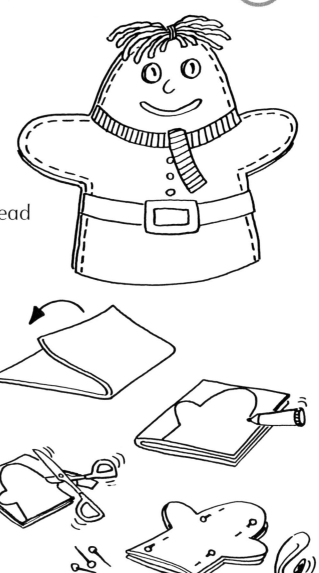

WHAT TO DO

1 Fold the felt in half.

2 Draw the shape of your glove puppet onto the felt.

3 Cut it out carefully.

4 Put in some pins to stop the felt moving.

5 Sew around the edges of the puppet with a back stitch or a blanket stitch. Remember to leave the bottom open for your hand!

6 Draw the face with marker pens.

7 Decorate the body in any way you like.

8 Have fun with your puppet!

How to make beans on toast for supper

Always get a grown-up to help you when you are cooking!

YOU WILL NEED

- 2 slices of bread

- tin of beans

- toaster

- tin opener

- saucepan

- wooden spoon

- plate

- knife and fork

WHAT TO DO

1 Open the tin of beans and pour the beans into a saucepan.

2 Heat the beans slowly on the cooker. Stir them a few times with the wooden spoon so they do not stick to the bottom.

3 Meanwhile, put the bread in the toaster to cook.

4 Put the toast on the plate and pour the beans over the top.

5 Enjoy your supper!

ANNOTATED VERSION – MODEL 1

TITLE –
To give purpose
of writing.

SIDE HEADING
– Introducing
list.

Numbered
points.

"To stop the
felt moving." –
To help the
reader
understand
why it is
important.

Warning to
avoid mistake.

ENDING –
Comment to
the reader.

How to make a puppet

WHAT YOU NEED

- a piece of felt
- pins
- marker pens
- large needle and coloured thread
- ribbons, buttons and wool for decoration
- scissors

WHAT TO DO

1 Fold[1] the felt in half.
2 Draw[1] the shape of your glove puppet onto the felt.
3 Cut[1] it out carefully.
4 Put[1] in some pins to stop the felt moving.
5 Sew[1] around the edges of the puppet with a back stitch or a blanket stitch. Remember to leave the bottom open for your hand!
6 Draw[1] the face with marker pens.
7 Decorate[1] the body in any way you like.
8 Have fun with your puppet!

DIAGRAM –
To make writing
clearer.

Key:
[1] "Bossy" verbs.

Pictures to make
the instructions
clearer.

93

How to make beans on toast for supper

Always get a grown-up to help you when you are cooking!

YOU WILL NEED

- 2 slices of bread
- tin of beans
- toaster
- tin opener
- saucepan
- wooden spoon
- plate
- knife and fork

WHAT TO DO

1 Open[1] the tin of beans and pour the beans into a saucepan.

2 Heat[1] the beans slowly on the cooker. Stir them a few times with the wooden spoon so they do not stick to the bottom.

3 Meanwhile, put[1] the bread in the toaster to cook.

4 Put[1] the toast on the plate and pour the beans over the top.

5 Enjoy your supper!

Key:
[1] "Bossy" verbs.

"So they do not stick to the bottom" – to help the reader understand that it is important to do this.

94

ORAL ACTIVITIES

1. Play games in the classroom or in the school grounds to give children practice at instructions for direction. Use words like: left, right, straight ahead, etc.

2. While teaching the unit, carry out lots of oral activities which relate to your school routine. Children will then get lots of practice in the formal tone needed before they write anything down.

E.g. ***How to come into class properly***

1. Hang up all coats and bags.

2. Put reading folders in the pile.

3. Sit in your place.

3. **Bossy Verb fun**

Give children a "long and polite" instruction.

They have to change it to a quick one that "bosses".

E.g. *Would you please put all the paints on your table away.*

Put the paints on the table away.

1. Can you find it?

As a follow up to the oral activities, let the children work in pairs to write a simple set of instructions from one place to another within the school.

To add to the fun, you could use a "treasure" theme and get the children to hide a small object at the finishing point.

The instructions should then be given to another pair who have to follow them. Will they find the treasure?

2. Have fun with fiction

Encourage imaginative thinking with short "fiction-based" tasks:

▶ How to keep your dragon happy.

▶ How to make a magic potion.

▶ Instructions to Little Red Riding Hood from her Mum.

3. Cook–in

Let the children work in groups on a simple task such as making a jam sandwich. Before they start, they must list what they need and only those things are provided! They can check the list and make changes as they go along. The group should write one version of the instructions for someone else to follow.

4. How to make a snowman

YOU WILL NEED

....

....

....

....

....

....

WHAT TO DO

....

....

....

....

....

....

WRITER'S TOOLKIT – INSTRUCTIONS

1 Give your work a title which makes the purpose of the instructions clear.

2 You can use side headings. They may be different for different sorts of instructions. For example: instructions about how to get somewhere will not usually need a "What you need" section.

3 Write a list of points, one under the other.

4 Write in an order. Numbers can be used. You could also use a flow chart.

5 Each point should be as short and clear as possible though may need to include advice to help the reader: *Stir them a few times with a wooden spoon so they do not stick to the bottom.*

6 Use the "bossy" part of the verb: *mix, stir, turn left.*

7 Draw a picture or diagram if it helps to make your writing clear.

SHORT TASKS

I put newspaper on my table. Next I filled the dish with red paint. I put my hand into the dish until it was covered with paint. Finally, I made a handprint on the piece of paper.

Turn this short recount into a set of instructions.

You need:

A TITLE

WHAT YOU NEED

....

....

....

....

....

WHAT TO DO

....

....

....

....

....

....

....

LONG TASKS

1 How to find the pirate treasure

WHAT YOU NEED

....

....

....

....

WHAT TO DO

....

....

....

....

....

....

....

....

LONG TASKS

2 How to grow seeds on a window sill

WHAT YOU NEED

....

....

....

....

WHAT TO DO

Draw pictures to show how to grow seeds on a window sill.

Write an instruction under each picture.

1	2

3	4

TEACHER'S NOTES

Young children enjoy reading about animals and fascination about creatures provides endless report writing material. Reports can also be written about school and the local area.

Read as a writer

1. Read and discuss the report about hedgehogs. Ask the children to discuss the type of writing and think about why it might have been written and who might read it.

2. Draw round each of the paragraphs and ask the children what each group of sentences is about. Establish that it does not matter what order the paragraphs are in. (One way to do this is to write paragraph headings on cards and get the children to organise them.)

3. Discuss the other features of the text. Where possible, use questioning to draw out the features. Let the children problem solve. Point out that the writer does not say "I" or "you" but writes about "hedgehogs". Although it is still perfectly acceptable for small children to write in that more informal way, it is, nevertheless, important to show them a formal model.

4. Can the children spot if the verbs are the same as they use in stories? Does it sound as though this is about hedgehogs in the past, or about hedgehogs now. This can be a way into the vexed question of tense.

5. Ask the children to spot the words which are to do with hedgehogs and their lives. Explain that these are included to give real facts.

6. Put all these features together into a Toolkit for writing.

Oral and Practice activities

7. These are designed to give children experience using certain language features and aspects of organisation of a non-chronological report. They can be used at any time to support the sequence of learning.

Writing

8. Use the 'Writer's Toolkit' and "model" another report about a hamster. It would be a good idea to demonstrate making notes about the hamster first. Children could be asked to do the same about another animal. In this way they are being taught about how to plan. Use the notes and the 'Writer's Toolkit' and explain the thinking behind the writing as a running commentary. You could split the demonstration into sections and ask the children to write about their animal after you have modelled each part.

9. The children could finally try the short and long assessment tasks.

Hedgehogs

A hedgehog is a small animal. It is nocturnal. This means it is awake at night time.

Hedgehogs have small pointy faces. Their bodies are covered with spines. When they are happy, the spines are flat against their back.

Hedgehogs eat insects, worms, snails and birds' eggs.

They live in woodland but they also live in people's gardens. In the winter, hedgehogs sometimes curl up inside piles of rubbish. They sleep through the winter though they often wake up if it is a warm day. They will find something to eat and then go back to sleep.

There are now not so many places for hedgehogs to live safely.

Hamsters

A hamster is a small animal.

Hamsters can have long or short hair. They can be lots of different colours such as cream, golden or brown.

The hamster needs a cage. Some cages have lots of tubes that fit together. They make rooms and passages and the hamsters get exercise moving around. Hamsters like playing on wheels inside their cage.

Hamsters like seeds, fruit, raw vegetables and cabbage or lettuce leaves. They often fill the pouches at the sides of their mouth with food and take it back to their bed.

Hamsters are often awake in the evening and at night. Sometimes they get cross if they get woken up to play in the day.

Hamsters make good pets.

ANNOTATED VERSION – MODEL 1

Hedgehogs

INTRODUCTION

A hedgehog is[1] a small animal. It is nocturnal[2]. This means it is awake at night time.

APPEARANCE

Hedgehogs have[1] small pointy faces. Their bodies are covered with spines[2]. When they are happy, the spines are flat against their back.

FOOD

Hedgehogs eat[1] insects, worms, snails and birds' eggs[2].

HABITAT

They live[1] in woodland[2] but they also live in people's gardens. In the winter, hedgehogs sometimes curl[1] up inside piles of rubbish. They sleep through the winter though they often wake up if it is a warm day. They will find something to eat and then go back to sleep.

**ENDING –
a general
comment.**

There are now not so many places for hedgehogs to live safely.

Key:
1 Some of the examples of present tense.

2 Words related to the subject of hedgehogs.

Hamsters

INTRODUCTION

A hamster is[1] a small animal.

APPEARANCE

Hamsters can have long or short hair. They can be lots of different colours such as cream, golden or brown[2].

CAGES

The hamster needs[1] a cage[2]. Some cages have lots of tubes[2] that fit together. They make rooms and passages and the hamsters get exercise moving around. Hamsters like[1] playing on wheels[2] inside their cage.

FOOD

Hamsters like seeds, fruit, raw vegetables and cabbage or lettuce leaves[2]. They often fill[1] the pouches[2] at the sides of their mouth with food and take it back to their bed.

WHEN THEY WAKE

Hamsters are often awake in the evening and at night. Sometimes they get cross if they get woken up to play in the day.

ENDING –
a general
comment.

Hamsters make[1] good pets[2].

Key:
1 Some examples of present tense.

2 Words related to topic of hamsters.

ORAL ACTIVITIES

1. Questions

Collecting information for a non-chronological report often involves asking questions.

Practise oral questions and ask the children to give a clear statement as an answer. Use the texts they have read as a starting point.

E.g. *What do hedgehogs eat?*
Do hamsters make good pets?

Next, use topics around the classroom and school that can be covered through observation or by going out of school to a park or playground.

You could turn this into a game by producing question word cards.

WHERE?	**WHAT?**	**WHEN?**
WHY?	**HOW?**	**WHO?**

One child could pick a card and make up a question for another to answer.

2. Give a talk

Let the children find out about topics that interest them and then give a very short talk to the class.

Other children could then ask questions to find out more.

PRACTICE ACTIVITIES

1. Labels

This activity works best if it is carried out as a class first.

Use a picture of an animal in a big book. If possible, find an unusual one. Prepare some small pieces of card with blu-tak on the back. Brainstorm the appearance of the creature with the children. Concentrate on getting correct names for parts of the body and clear descriptive words. Write the suggestions on the card and stick them next to the features.

Provide more pictures for pairs to work on together.

2. From labels to paragraph

Demonstrate how to turn the labels that the class came up with in the previous activity into three or four sentences about the appearance of the animals.

Children can then do the same activity individually or in pairs. It will be necessary for the teacher to act as scribe for the least able who will still be working on creating oral sentences.

3. An imaginary animal

Demonstrate this activity before the children begin.

Work in pairs to draw and colour an imaginary animal. Label it. This can then be turned into a description.

This activity could be extended with further pages about food, habitat, etc. Each page could have a picture and a small paragraph.

The work could be turned into a group or class book. If this is done, the children could make a contents page and include any other non-fiction book features that they have already studied.

4. Vocabulary brainstorm

Assuming that the children might be writing short reports about pets, help to prepare them by brainstorming activities to develop vocabulary.

WHAT DOES IT LOOK LIKE?

DESCRIPTION – SIZE?

        TEXTURE?

        COLOUR?

        SHAPE?

WHAT ARE THE PARTS OF ITS BODY?

WHAT DOES IT EAT?

WHERE DOES IT LIVE?

WHAT DOES IT DO?

WRITER'S TOOLKIT – NON-CHRONOLOGICAL REPORTS

▶ Start with a short sentence to say what the writing is about.

▶ Write sentences about the same topic together in paragraphs.

▶ Write a sentence at the end to finish off the report.

▶ Use present tense. Write as though things are happening at the moment. *The hamster needs a cage* NOT *The hamster needed a cage.*

▶ Do not use names of people or animals.

▶ Include detail about the subject, e.g. *information about where hedgehogs live.*

▶ Do not use "I" or "we" in the writing.

1 Looking after me

Choose one of the things you do to look after yourself and write a short paragraph about it.

2 Other people who help me

Choose one of the sections above. Write about what the person does and how they can help people.

LONG TASKS

My town

Imagine that you had to describe your town to a visitor in another country. Use the boxes to plan ideas and write a few sentences about each section.

Badger Publishing Limited
26 Wedgwood Way, Pin Green Industrial Estate,
Stevenage, Hertfordshire SG1 4QF
Telephone: 01438 356907
Fax: 01438 747015
www.badger-publishing.co.uk
enquiries@badger-publishing.co.uk

Badger Test Revision Guides
Key Stage 1 English
Teacher Book with Copymasters
ISBN 1 84424 265 X

Publisher: David Jamieson
Editor: Paul Martin
Designer: Lodestone Publishing Limited   www.lodestonepublishing.com
Illustrators: Martha Hardy, Jon Mitchell, Lorraine White

Printed in the UK.